The Book of Monologues for Aspiring Actors

The Book of

Monologues
for Aspiring
Actors

Marsh Cassady

Glencoe

New York, New York   Columbus, Ohio   Chicago, Illinois   Peoria, Illinois   Woodland Hills, California

In memory of Reverend Robert Rau

Cover photo: from a production of *The Importance of Being Earnest,* courtesy of San Diego City Schools, California.

Acknowledgments for interior photos and dramatic selections are listed on page 211, which represents a continuation of the copyright page.

The McGraw·Hill Companies

Send all Inquiries to:
Glencoe/McGraw-Hill
8787 Orion Place
Columbus, OH 43240

ISBN : 0-8442-5771-0
Printed in the United States of America
7 8 9 10 11 12 <u>045</u> 08 07 06 05 04

Contents

Introduction

The Book of Monologues for Aspiring Actors was written to acquaint young people with a diversity of one-person scenes, which they can use for a variety of purposes. The first purpose of these scenes is to acquaint them with the language and thought of many different writers throughout history, thus providing a springboard for the study of the periods, the playwrights, and the drama. Second, the scenes can be used as practice for those interested in learning and developing skills in acting and/or directing. They can help in developing character and learning about movement, voice, and placement. Third, the monologues can provide material for those interested in participating in oral interpretation contests and presentations. Finally, because nearly all the monologues are delivered by characters between the ages of twelve and twenty-one, students will have a chance to play roles close to their own ages, which may have more relevance for them than would scenes with older or younger characters.

The scenes range in length from one minute to nearly fifteen minutes. If they so wish, students can start with shorter scenes requiring less time for memorization, and then work up gradually to the longer scenes.

Of course, those who want to participate in district or state oral interpretation contests will want to choose the longer monologues to match the requirements. That is the major reason the book includes so many more modern and contemporary monologues than those from other historical periods. Most longer scenes appear in recent theatrical presentations, and they often come across better as interpretive pieces than do historical pieces. This is because the historical pieces often require a different manner of speaking and deal with different beliefs and social mores.

The majority of the longer monologues come from complete plays, though there are several that are meant to stand alone and are illustrative of a trend in recent years toward *performance pieces* rather than drama with a specific set of characters. This newer type of theatre has its roots in Greek drama, then in medieval religious drama that was meant to instruct, and later in the *commedia dell'arte* with its emphasis on current issues. A performance piece relies on a blending of many elements including dance, film, video, singing, photos and so on, all of which may be related only in that they deal with a particular theme, such as ecology or child abuse. A few of the monologues in this collection are taken from nondramatic sources, such as short stories or novels.

In the introduction to each monologue the time range is listed. Students should not worry if the piece is somewhat longer or shorter than the suggested range since everyone's delivery will be different.

The pieces were chosen so that with a short introduction they can stand alone. For a few of the longer monologues various stopping places are given, so that the presentation, if desired, can take seven minutes, for example, or be lengthened one or two minutes more. Also, suggestions are given on how the monologue can be cut to fit better into a shorter time limitation.

In some instances, speeches have been combined and other characters' responses appear in brackets. Most often, the student has a choice of presenting the scene as though other characters actually are present. In one or two instances, it will be necessary to play to characters who are there only in the imagination.

Introductions to each monologue will set the scene and explain the context. Particularly in oral interpretation situations, the student may want to incorporate the information into a verbal scene setting.

Just as each person in life approaches a situation or encounter in a different way, so too will students interpret and react individually to each scene. There is no right or wrong way of presenting the scenes. There are as many "correct" interpretations as there are students. There *are* correct rules of presentation, such as projecting the voice so everyone in the classroom or audience can hear the monologue. The monologues will provide practice using these rules. But in addition to learning how to act or give a reading, students should receive enjoyment and satisfaction from each monologue they choose to present. Theatre, after all, is for enjoyment and entertainment.

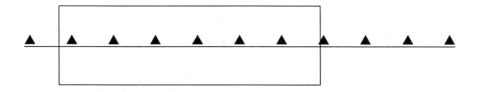

Preparing Your Monologues

Since there is a wide variety of styles and historical periods represented in *The Book of Monologues for Aspiring Actors*, you should take your time choosing the monologues that you know you will enjoy staying with over a period of time. Because you will be working very closely over a period of days or even weeks with each monologue you choose, you will want to select one that you will continue to like. Of course, your instructor may give you certain requirements, such as choosing a piece from a particular historical period or of a specific length. Even so, you will have several monologues from which to select. A chart at the end of the book lists each monologue and gives the name and age of the character, and the length of time the scene should take. The times are approximate.

It is usually better not to choose too quickly or impulsively. Rather, read over all the monologues that fit your assignment. Then decide which of these you like. Wait a day or two and approach the monologue with a fresh mind. If you still like it as much as you did at first, go ahead with it. If not, choose something different.

Analyzing the Monologue

Although the steps in analyzing the piece you've selected are listed in sequence, often you will find that they overlap. For example, it often is difficult to figure out what the piece means without knowing the character who is speaking. The steps that follow show the sorts of things you need to consider, but you may choose to do them in a different order. To help you with this, there is an analysis sheet that you or your teacher may want to photocopy (p. 7). It can help guide you in giving an effective performance when you appear before your audience.

1. Once your selection is final, the next step is to determine why you like the monologues. Is it because you identify with the character or agree with what he or she is saying? Or maybe you like the humor or the mood. Once you know why you are drawn to the piece, you can try to convey that same feeling to an audience.

2. What is the mood of the piece? Is it comic or serious? Does it deal with an important subject, and how does the subject affect the mood? This, of course, is tied in with the character's feelings. From what the character is saying, can you figure out how the person feels?

3. Determine the theme of the monologue, that is, the central idea or what the writer is saying through the character. What does the writer most want to say to an audience?

4. Before getting too far along in the preparation of the monologue, you need to analyze your character and to determine important aspects that will help you portray the person better and so make your presentation more effective. Here are some of the elements you should consider.

   a. Where is the character from? How does this affect feelings, thoughts, and attitudes?

   b. How old is the character? How can you effectively portray a person this age? If the person is younger or older than you, how should you go about portraying him or her?

   c. What can you tell about the character's environment—geographically, historically, and economically? What is the social status of the individual? How does all this affect the type of person he or she is?

   d. Similarly, what have been and what are the major influences on the person's life? Sometimes this is easy to determine because the entire monologue relates to an issue important to the person. Sometimes, you can only infer specifics about the character.

e. What are the character's personality traits? How can you tell? How do the traits affect how the person comes across in the monologue?

f. What are the character's motives and goals? What does the person hope to accomplish, as far as you can tell by what is said in the monologue? Why is he or she reaching for this goal?

g. Is the person likable? Why or why not? How do you feel about the character? What makes you feel this way?

5. The next step is planning the presentation, and for this you need to take into consideration everything that you have discovered while doing the analysis. Using this information, you can approach this part of your presentation in whatever way you like. For instance, some actors like to memorize the text before working out movement and gestures; others like to put everything together at the same time. Do whatever you think will work better for you.

a. Memorizing the monologue is an individual process, so what may work well for someone else might not work for you. (1) Make sure you know the meaning of each word and phrase. Although this is important for every type of monologue, you may have to do more investigating of the meanings of words and references in historical pieces. (2) Memorize the ideas and the flow of the monologue so that you have the outline or the ideas firmly in mind before you try to memorize exact words. (3) Often it is better to first memorize one sentence and then memorize a second, which you add to the first. As you move through the monologue, keep adding a sentence at a time and repeating the entire procedure for each new sentence. (4) Work on memorizing the monologue as the last thing before you go to sleep at night; this helps you retain it.

b. Plan the movement and gestures. If you are the type of person who normally uses a lot of gestures and movement in everyday life, you probably will use more in presenting your monologue. Of course, you should be guided by several things: (1) the type of person the character is; (2) how you interpret the emotional situation that either calls for more movement, as anger or nervousness might, or less movement, as fright could; (3) any special requirements or restrictions that go along with your purpose in presenting the monologue, such as relying more on voice usage in some oral interpretation situations.

6. You need to practice the piece so you can be sure of presenting it to the best of your ability. Part of this is just going over and over the piece until you are sure you have it firmly fixed in your mind. But then you might want to use an audio recorder so you can listen to your voice and judge whether you're getting across the feelings and ideas that you want. You also may want to practice in front of a mirror to judge your movement and gestures. If you have access to a video camera, you may want to have someone tape your monologue so that you can both look at it and listen to it and better evaluate how the presentation is coming across. Like memorization, practice is an individual thing, so it's best to experiment to see what works best for you. For instance, some people may find it helpful to give a few "dry runs" in front of friends or family to get their reactions; others would feel that this may be too inhibiting.

7. You need to plan an introduction, rather than relying on inspiration when you are up in front of your classmates or another audience. There are several elements you might want to include.

   a. In doing a piece from a large work, you certainly will want to tell the audience anything about the play, the playwright, the historical period, or where your scene fits in so they can better understand and appreciate the performance. Set the scene for the audience so they can feel they are a part of the presentation.

   b. Depending on the circumstances, you might tell the audience why you chose the monologue and what it means to you. Maybe it expresses a strong belief of yours or you find it relevant to your life.

   c. Usually, except occasionally for some oral interpretation events, the introduction should not be more than ninety seconds or so. Your major purpose is to give a monologue, not a talk.

Analysis Sheet

Play or monologue title _____

Writer _____

Why I like this monologue _____
_____

Theme or what the monologue means to me _____
_____

_____

Overall mood _____

My Character

    Where from _____

    Age _____

    Environment _____

    Major influences _____

    Personality traits _____

    Motives and goals _____

    How I feel about the character _____

Information to Include in the Introduction

    About the monologues _____

    Why I chose it _____

    What it means to me _____

Monologues
for Females

Agamemnon

Iphigenia in Aulis

Antigone

Playing time: Four minutes and 15 seconds to four minutes and 45 seconds

Character's age: About 20

Agamemnon

Aeschylus/ *Greece*

This play, written in 458 B.C., is the first in a trilogy that deals with the subject of justice. The tragedy opens with a watchman looking for the beacon fires that will announce the fall of Troy.

It becomes clear through his dialogue and that of the chorus, which plays a large part in the drama, that Clytemnestra has been unfaithful to Agamemnon, the king and her husband.

Agamemnon enters with Cassandra—a captive princess and a prophet. In this scene Cassandra foretells her own death and Agamemnon's, both at the hands of Clytemnestra, who shortly afterwards catches them both in a net and stabs them to death.

For a better understanding of the conditions of the play and the time it was written, it would be helpful to read about ancient Greek (classical) theatre in general and Aeschylus and his plays in particular.

CASSANDRA:
   It comes—it comes. Oh, misery.
   The awful pain of prophecy—it comes,
   a whirling wind of madness.
   See them—those yonder by the wall—there—there—
   so young—like forms that hover in a dream.
   Children they seem—murdered by those they loved.
   And in their hands is flesh—It is their own.
   And inward parts—Oh, load most horrible.
   I see it—and their father made his feast—
   Vengeance, I say, from these is shaping still—
   a lion's shape,[1] who never fights, who lurks
   within a bed, until the master comes—
   The master? Mine. The slave's yoke. I must bear it.
   Lord of the ships who laid waste Ilium—
   and yet not know that she-wolf's tongue.
   She licks her lord's hand—fawns with pricking ear,
   and bites at last, like secret death.

   Such daring has a woman to kill a man?
   How name her? Evil beast, a snake,
   the monster crouching on the shore to prey on sailors,
   the mother of hell, mad-raging, wild to war,
   implacable, against her very own.
   Her cry of joy—oh, woman daring all things,
   joyful as men shout when the battle turns.
   Her show of triumph for his home-coming—
   Believe or not. Why do I longer care?
   The thing that is to be shall be. And you
   here standing, soon will in your pity call me
   a prophet all too true.
[LEADER: How once a father feasted on his children,
   those words I understand, cold to my heart.
   And terror holds me when she speaks no fancies
   but what I know. All else she says I hear—
   no more, I have no clue.]

CASSANDRA: Then hear the truth.
   Your eyes shall look on Agamemnon dead.

---

[1] She is referring to Clytemnestra's lover, son of the man who was forced to feast on his own children.

[AN OLD MAN: Peace, wretched girl. Hush on your lips those words.]

CASSANDRA: No peace is on my lips.

[ANOTHER: If it must be—O God, not so—not so.]

CASSANDRA: You pray. Their care is death.

[ANOTHER: Who? Who is he who plots this cursed thing?]

CASSANDRA: You will not read my prophecy aright.

[ANOTHER: Because I know the deed could not be done.]

CASSANDRA: And yet I speak the Greek tongue—all too well.

[ANOTHER: Greek are the oracles but none can read them.]

CASSANDRA: Oh, strange! A flame—moving—It comes upon me.
Oh, terrible! Apollo! I see—I see—
A lioness—that walks upon two feet—
a wolf she lies with, the royal lion gone.
It is she will kill me. Pity me.
She brews a poison, and she swears
the vial of her wrath holds death for me.
I too must die because he brought me hither.
Her plan—and while she whets her sword for him.
Why then these gaudy things on head and throat?
They mock at me—the prophet's wreaths—the staff.
Down with you—now, before I die myself. Begone.

[*She tears off the adornments that mark her a prophet and stamps on them*]

You fall, and I myself shall follow soon.
Make rich in woe some other woman now.
See now. It is Apollo who has stripped me,
taken his prophet's robe. He watched while I was mocked,
still in his livery, reviled by friends
turned foes—one voice—no reason—to them all,
calling me vagrant, mountebank, a cheat,
a beggar. Wretched and starving I endured
The prophet now has done with me, his prophet.
It is he has brought me to this pass of death.

They slew my father on an altar stone.
For me a block waits hot with murdered blood.
Surely we shall not die unmarked of God.

Another[2] to avenge will come in turn,
to slay the one who bore him, to exact
blood for a father's blood. A wanderer,
outcast from home, he shall return at last
and crown the sins that blindly doomed his race.
A great oath has been sworn of God most high.
The fallen helpless corpse shall lead him home.
But I—why weep and pity such as these?
I, who once saw the town of Ilium
fare as she fared. And they that cast her down
have thus their end in the decrees of God.
So now I go to end as they have done.
I will endure to die. O gates of death,
my greeting. But—pray God, the blow strike home
quickly. No struggle. Death coming easily.
Blood ebbing gently and my eyes then closed.

Questions

1. What is the predominant mood of the scene? What emotions is Cassandra feeling? How might you try to convey these emotions?

2. Do you feel that the action of the play is believable? Why? How do you suppose the ancient Greeks would have reacted to this scene? Why?

3. Do you think it's true-to-life that Agamemnon has brought home the princess Cassandra? Or that Clytemnestra has been unfaithful? Why?

4. Why do you think Clytemnestra kills Agamemnon and Cassandra?

5. Do you like this monologue? Why?

---

[2] Orestes later returns and kills Clytemnestra, his mother, because she killed his father.

Playing time: Two minutes to two minutes and
15 seconds
Character's age: 18 to 20

Iphigenia in Aulis

Euripides/*Greece*

Euripides wrote this play about 405 B.C. Unlike other
playwrights of the Classical Age, he dealt with specific emotions and social issues as related to individuals rather than to
the community as a whole.

Agamemnon and Clytemnestra again appear in this play,
since writers of Greek tragedy based their characters on
figures from familiar myths.

In *Iphigenia in Aulis,* Agamemnon, unable to sail from
Aulis because of wayward winds, has been informed by the
oracle (a giver of prophecies from the gods) that he will not
be able to capture Troy unless he sacrifices his daughter
Iphigenia. Under pressure from his army and his brother
Menelaus, he sends for her on the pretext that she is to marry
Achilles.

Later he has a change of heart and sends a message to
Clytemnestra, his wife, to keep Iphigenia at home. Menelaus
intercepts the message. The two men are quarreling when the
women arrive.

After more conflict and argument among the men,
Iphigenia announces that she is resolved to die for Greece.
Following is the speech she gives.

IPHIGENIA:
> Listen, mother, listen.
> You know nothing can change
> What is going to happen.
> I must die. And I want it.
>
> My father was right: on me depends
> The sailing of the ships
>
> And the defeat of Troy.
> What is so precious
> About this life of mine?
> I give my mortal self
> To Greece for sacrifice
> To destroy our enemies.
> This will be my monument
> In times to come. This
> Will be my children. This
> Will be my marriage. This,
> This will be my fame.
>
> Remember what they say:
> Men, and women too,
> Must endure. I say
> An old, worn, ancient thing
> And yet it is a true thing.
> Nothing's new or changes
> But each of us must learn
> To discover it anew.
> You must not weep.
> I am happy, dying.
> Life is brief and brutish.
> By how we live we make it
> Have a little meaning
> And have a little brightness,
> As light braves the darkness . . .
> O I love you very much.
>
> Take from me a lock of hair
> And let's have no more weeping.
> Fetch me my wedding veil
> And give me wreaths to wind
> Around my head. Bring them.
>
> You are now my women.
> You shall come with me and dance

Around Artemis' altar.
Let us praise and honour her
And dance the wedding dance.
I give myself to her.
If Achilles had married me
I should have been given
To hot Aphrodite
As other women are.
But I will worship Artemis
And so I will be free
Clean and bright and strong.
I am the bride now
Of Greece. I love you. Take me.
Take me. I am conqueror
Of Troy, of Ilion.[1]
Come women, sing,
Sing to Artemis,
Protector of travellers
and of the army waiting.

Now sing of my country's earth
And of my home, Mycenae.

Questions

1. Why do you think Iphigenia is so willing to go to her death? In light of the time in which the play was written, do you think the audience would have considered this logical? Why?

2. What does Iphigenia say about life? Why do you think she says this? Do you agree with her?

3. What do you think of Agamemnon's decision to sacrifice his daughter? Is it logical that he would do it?

4. How does Iphigenia feel about dying for Greece? She tells her mother she knows it has to happen. Why do you think she says this?

5. Why does Iphigenia tell the others not to weep for her? If you were witnessing this scene, how would you feel about it? Why?

---

[1] Another name for Troy; Ilus was the city's founder.

Antigone

Sophocles / *Greece*

*A*ntigone was first produced in 41 B.C. when Sophocles, often considered the most skillful of the Greek dramatists, was in his mid-fifties. He wrote psychological dramas in which the central character is forced to examine his or her own beliefs and values. Because of this, the characters come across as more human than those of other writers of the time.

Antigone begins after a battle in which the city of Thebes has triumphed but lost its king. The new king, Creon, decrees that the body of Polyneices, who led the invasion, is to remain unburied. Just afterward, Creon is told that the princess Antigone, sister of Polyneices and niece of Creon, has tried to bury the body.

Antigone makes no effort to hide what she's done and even challenges Creon's right to issue the decree, saying it goes against the will of the gods. As a result, Creon sentences Antigone to be entombed alive.

Creon's son, Antigone's fiancé, pleads with his father to save Antigone's life. He flees distraught when Creon refuses his request. Next the old prophet Tiresias urges Creon to reconsider both the decree about Polyneices and the sentence he's given Antigone.

Tiresias says that great misfortune will fall upon Creon if he doesn't change this decree. Terrified, Creon rushes off to bury Polyneices and free Antigone. But he's too late.

Antigone's speech comes just before she kills herself, after which Creon's son does the same.

ANTIGONE:
> O tomb, O marriage-chamber, hollowed out
> house that will watch forever, where I go.
>
> To my own people, who are mostly there;
> Persephone has taken them to her.
> Last of them all, ill-fated past the rest,
> shall I descend, before my course is run.
> Still when I get there I may hope to find
> I come as a dear friend to my dear father,
> to you, my mother, and my brother too.
> All three of you have known my hand in death.
> I washed your bodies, dressed them for the grave,
> poured out the last libation at the tomb.
> Last, Polyneices knows the price I pay
> for doing final service to his corpse.
> And yet the wise will know my choice was right.
> Had I had children or their father dead,
> I'd let them moulder. I should not have chosen
> in such a case to cross the state's decree.
> What is the law that lies behind these words?
> One husband gone, I might have found another,
> or a child from a new man in first child's place,
> but with my parents hid away in death,
> no brother, ever, could spring up for me.
> Such was the law by which I honored you.
> But Creon thought the doing was a crime,
> a dreadful daring, brother of my heart.
> So now he takes and leads me out by force.
> No marriage-bed, no marriage-song for me,
> and since no wedding, so no child to rear.
> I go, without a friend, struck down by fate,
> live to the hollow chambers of the dead.
> What divine justice have I disobeyed?
> Why, in my misery, look to the gods for help?
> Can I call any of them my ally?
> I stand convicted of impiety,
> the evidence my pious duty done.
> Should the gods think that this is righteousness,
> in suffering I'll see my error clear.
> But if it is the others who are wrong
> I wish them no greater punishment than mine.

Questions

1. Why do you suppose Creon decreed that Polyneices' body should not be buried?

2. Why do you think Antigone defies the decree? What would you do in similar circumstances? Explain.

3. What can you tell from the speech about the type of person Antigone is?

4. Do you think you would like to see this play or appear in it? Why?

5. How would you describe Antigone's emotional state while delivering this speech? Explain.

Monologues
for Males

The Libation Bearers

Hippolytus

The Persians

Playing time: Two minutes and 20 seconds to two minutes and 40 seconds
Character's age: 18 to 20

The Libation Bearers

Aeschylus/*Greece*

This is the second play in a trilogy. The first, *Agamemnon,* retells the murder of the king Agamemnon. *The Libation Bearers* tells how Agamemnon's children carry out vengeance against their mother, Clytemnestra, who had justified the murder of her husband because of his sacrifice of their daughter Iphagenia to appease the gods, thus allowing him to sail into battle against Troy. The three plays, interconnected so much that they really are just acts of one long play, show how the concept of justice evolves, with the power of the state finally replacing personal revenge.

Orestes, Agamemnon's son, returns home and lays a lock of hair as an offering on his father's tomb. That night, his sister Electra comes to pray at the tomb and discovers the hair. The two are united, and Orestes tells her his plan to avenge his father's death.

This speech shows Orestes' feelings about what his mother has done.

ORESTES:

See there, the two princes[1] of this land.
They killed my father, plundered the house.
They were solemn as they sat on their thrones.
They are dear friends to one another still—

(*He points at the two bodies.*)

so at least you would think from how they are now.
Their plighted oath stands fast still, which they swore
to work the murder of my wretched father
and die themselves, together.
Yes, they have kept their oaths well.
And look you, now, those that have heard
the sad story,

(*He holds up an imaginary robe.*)

look at the traps for my poor father,
the tyings of his feet,
the fetters of his hands, the linkage of his legs.
Spread the garment out, and show it to all that stand
around here: this was the covering of the man.
Let the father see it—not my father, of course,
but the father that looks down upon
all that is done here, the Sun-Father.
These are the deeds, the filthy deeds, of my mother;
let them be a testimony to Justice, one day,
that this murder which I have done
was justly done; my mother's murder.
(I do not even speak about Aegisthus and his death;
he had what is legally come to him,
the justice due to an adulterer.)
She it was who planned this hateful act upon him,
on him whose child she had carried heavy within her,
a child once loved but now, in the event,
a hating enemy.
How does she seem to you? Was she a viper,
or a sea serpent, whose very touch brings corruption
though the hand was not bitten? Shall we so call her,
for her bold and vicious spirit?
What shall I say of the robe? What shall I call it
and make the name good? Was it a snare

---

[1]Orestes is referring to his mother and her lover Aegisthus.

for a wild thing, or a covering for a corpse,
a bathrobe for him, trailing to his feet?
No, not a snare, but a net, you might say,
and a robe that fell to his feet.
Maybe the sort of thing a highwayman
might use, to make a living, robbing travelers;
with such equipment he might gladden his heart,
as he plundered many.
May never a woman like her share house of mine!
May the gods curse me rather to have no child!

Questions

1. Do you think it logical that a son could kill his mother? Why?

2. What are the reasons Orestes gives for killing Clytemnestra?

3. What can you tell from this scene about the kind of person Orestes is?

4. What part does the robe play in this scene? Why do you think Orestes refers to it?

5. How do you think Orestes feels about himself after he kills his mother? Why?

Playing time: Three minutes and 15 seconds to
three minutes and 45 seconds
Character's age: 18 to 19

Hippolytus

Euripides/ *Greece*

All his life Hippolytus has scorned the idea of sexual love
and the worship of Aphrodite and instead has devoted himself
to worshiping the chaste goddess Artemis.

To get back at him, the goddess Aphrodite causes his
stepmother, Phaedra, to have an overwhelming attraction to
him. Phaedra tries to resist by starving herself, but at the point
of dying she is coaxed into revealing to her nurse how she
feels.

The nurse in turn tells Hippolytus, who reacts so violently
that Phaedra can hear him shouting. To get revenge on him
for this, the stepmother leaves a message for her husband, the
king Tereseus, that Hippolytus did indeed violate her body.
She then hangs herself.

Tereseus places a curse on his son and exiles him. This is
Hippolytus' reaction.

HIPPOLYTUS:

Your mind and intellect are subtle, father:
here you have a subject dressed in eloquent words;
But if you lay the matter bare of words
the matter is not eloquent. I am
no man to speak with vapid, precious skill
before a mob, although among my equals
and in a narrow circle I am held
not unaccomplished in the eloquent art.
That is as it should be. The demagogue
who charms a crowd is scorned by cultured experts.
But here in this necessity I must speak.
First I shall take the argument you first
urged as so irrefutable and deadly.
You see the earth and air about you, father?
In all of that there lives no man more chaste
than I, though you deny it.
It is my rule to honour the Gods first
and then to have as friends only such men
as do no sin, nor offer wicked service
nor will consent to sin to serve a friend
as a return for kindness. I am no railer
at my companions. Those who are my friends
find me as much their friends when they are absent
as when we are together.

There is one thing that I have never done, the thing
of which you think that you convict me, father,
I am a virgin to this very day.
Save what I have heard or what I have seen in pictures
I'm ignorant of the deed. Nor do I wish
to see such things for I've a maiden soul.
But say you disbelieve my chastity.
Then tell me how it was *your* wife seduced me:
was it because she was more beautiful
than all the other women in the world?
Or did I think, when I had taken her,
to win your place and kingdom for a dowry
and live in your own house? I would have been
a fool, a senseless fool, if I had dreamed it.
Was rule so sweet? Never, I tell you, Theseus,
for the wise. A man whom power has so enchanted

must be demented. I would wish to be
first in the contests of the Hellenic Games
but in the city I'd take second place
and an enduring happy life among
the best society who are my friends.
So one has time to work and danger's absence
has charms above the royal diadem.
But a word more and my defence is finished.
If I had one more witness to my character,
if I were tried when *she* still saw the light,
deeds would have helped you as you scanned your friends
to know the true from the false. But now I swear,
I swear to you by Zeus, the god of oaths,
by this deep rooted fundament of earth,
I never sinned against you with your wife
nor would have wished or thought of it.
If I have been a villain may I die
unfamed, unknown, a homeless stateless beggar,
an exile! May the earth and sea refuse
to give my body rest when I am dead!
Whether your wife took her own life because
she was afraid, I do not know. I may not speak
further than this.
Virtuous she was in deed although not virtuous:
I that have virtue used it to my ruin.

Questions

1. How does Hippolytus describe himself? Why?

2. Why do you think Phaedra delivered the false message?

3. Why do you think Hippolytus has vowed to be chaste?

4. Is Hippolytus a believable person? Why?

5. Do you think it's logical that Phaedra killed herself when she heard Hippolytus' reaction to what the nurse told him? Why?

Playing time: Six minutes to six minutes and 30 seconds
Character's age: Probably 18 to 20

The Persians

Aeschylus/*Greece*

The chorus, made up of aged councilors of the Persian Empire, tell of the departure of their ruler Xerxes' expedition against Greece. They talk of their anxiety and how they long for news of the campaign. Queen Atossa, the widow of Darius and the mother of Xerxes, enters, bothered by an ominous dream.

A messenger arrives and tells of the defeat of the Persian fleet at Salamis and the subsequent disastrous retreat of the Persian land forces back to Asia.

MESSENGER:

   Some Fury, some malignant Power,
   Appeared, and set in train the whole disastrous rout.

   A Hellene from the Athenian army came and told
   Your son Xerxes this tale: that, once the shades of night
   Set in, the Hellenes would not stay, but leap on board,
   And, by whatever secret route offered escape,
   Row for their lives. When Xerxes heard this, with no thought
   Of the man's guile, or of the jealousy of the gods,
   He sent this word to all his captains: "When the sun
   No longer flames to warm the earth, and darkness holds
   The court of heaven, range the main body of our fleet
   Threefold, to guard the outlets and the choppy straits."
   Then he sent other ships to row right round the isle,
   Threatening that if the Hellene ships found a way through
   To save themselves from death, he would cut off the head
   Of every Persian captain. By these words he showed
   How ignorance of the gods' intent had dazed his mind.

   Our crews, then, in good order and obediently,
   Were getting supper; then each oarsman looped his oar
   To the smooth rowing-pin; and when the sun went down
   And night came on, the rowers all embarked, and all
   The heavy-armed soldiers; and from line to line they called,
   Cheering each other on, rowing and keeping course
   As they were ordered.
                                          All night long the captains kept
   Their whole force cruising to and fro across the strait.
   Now night was fading; still the Hellenes showed no sign
   Of trying to sail out unnoticed; till at last
   Over the earth shone the white horses of the day,
   Filling the air with beauty. Then from the Hellene ships
   Rose like a song of joy the piercing battle-cry,
   And from the island crags echoed an answering shout.

   The Persians knew their error; fear gripped every man.
   They were no fugitives who sang that terrifying
   Paean, but Hellenes charging with courageous hearts
   To battle. The loud trumpet flamed along their ranks.
   At once their frothy oars moved with a single pulse,
   Beating the salt waves to the bo'suns' chant; and soon
   Their whole fleet hove clear into view; their right wing first,
   In precise order, next their whole array came on,

And at that instant a great shout beat our ears:
"Forward, you sons of Hellas! Set your country free!
Set free your sons, your wives, tombs of your ancestors,
And temples of your gods. All is at stake: now fight!"
Then from our side in answer rose the manifold
Clamour of Persian voices; and the hour had come.

At once ship into ship battered its brazen beak.
A Hellene ship charged first, and chopped off the whole stern
Of a Phoenician galley. Then charge followed charge
On every side. At first by its huge impetus
Our fleet withstood them. But soon, in the narrow space,
Our ships were jammed in hundreds; none could help another.
They rammed each other with their prows of bronze; and some
Were stripped of every oar. Meanwhile the enemy
Came round us in a ring and charged. Our vessels heeled
Over; the sea was hidden, carpeted with wrecks
And dead men; all the shores and reefs were full of dead.

Then every ship we had broke rank and rowed for life.
The Hellenes seized fragments of wrecks and broken oars
And hacked and stabbed at our men swimming in the sea
As fishermen kill tunnies or some netted haul.
The whole sea was one din of shrieks and dying groans,
Till night and darkness hid the scene.

         If I should speak
For ten days and ten nights, I could not tell you all
That day's agony. But know this: never before
In one day died so vast a company of men.

But there is more, and worse.

         Opposite Salamis
There is an island—small, useless for anchorage—
Where Pan the dancer treads along the briny shore.
There Xerxes sent them, so that, when the enemy,
Flung from their ships, were struggling to the island beach,
The Persian force might without trouble cut them down,
And rescue Persian crews from drowning in the sea;
Fatal misjudgement!

       When in the sea-battle Heaven
Had given glory to the Hellenes, that same day
They came, armed with bronze shields and spears, leapt from their
  ships,
And made a ring round the whole island, that our men

Could not tell where to turn. First came a shower of blows
From stones slung with the hand; then from the drawn bowstring
Arrows leapt forth to slaughter; finally, with one
Fierce roar the Hellenes rushed at them, and cut and carved
Their limbs like butchers, till the last poor wretch lay dead.

The depth of horror Xerxes saw; close to the sea
On a high hill he sat, where he could clearly watch
His whole force both by sea and land. He wailed aloud,
And tore his clothes, weeping; and instantly dismissed
His army, hastening them to a disordered flight.

He who died quickest, was luckiest. The handful who survived,
Suffering untold hardship, struggled on through Thrace
To safety, and now at last have reached their native earth.

So, well may Persia's cities mourn their young men lost.
I have spoken truth; yet all I have told is but a part
Of all the evil God sent to strike Persia down.

Questions

1. How do you suppose the messenger feels about what happened to Xerxes' men? Explain.

2. What caused the defeat? Why does the messenger say that those who died early on were lucky?

3. In Greek theatre of the classical period, no violence was ever shown on stage. Why do you suppose it wasn't? Do you think it is better to tell of violence rather than show it? Why?

4. If you had to return to deliver a message such as this, what emotions would you feel? How do you think these compare to the emotions the messenger feels?

5. Do you feel sorry for the messenger? Why?

Monologues
for Females

Playing time: Two minutes and 25 seconds to two minutes and 45 seconds
Character's age: About 14

Romeo and Juliet

William Shakespeare / *England*

*R*omeo and Juliet, written in 1595, is one of the most well-known love stories in all of literature. Romeo and Juliet, who fall in love, are members of families on opposite sides of a feud. Still the two young people are married secretly by Friar Laurence, Romeo's friend, who hopes the marriage will put an end to the feud.

Later Romeo is forced into a fight, which he tries to avoid, and his best friend Mercutio is killed. Romeo in turns kills Tybalt, Juliet's cousin, and then takes refuge with Friar Laurence, his friend and religious confessor. In the meantime, Juliet's parents think she's grieving for Tybalt and try to alleviate her sorrow by insisting she marry another man named Paris.

Juliet consults Friar Laurence who advises her to seem to agree to the marriage and then gives her a sleeping potion which for a time will make it appear as if she's dead. Instead of being married, she'll be taken to the family's burial vault. By the time she awakens, Romeo will have time to return and take her away.

In this scene, Juliet is about to take the potion.

JULIET:

Farewell! God knows when we shall meet again.
I have a faint cold fear thrills through my veins
That almost freezes up the heat of life.
I'll call them back again to comfort me.
Nurse!—What should she do here?
My dismal scene I needs must act alone.
Come, vial.
What if this mixture do not work at all?
Shall I be married then tomorrow morning?
No, no, this shall forbid it. Lie thou there.

(Laying down a dagger.)

What if it be a poison which the Friar
Subtly hath ministered[1] to have me dead,
Lest in this marriage he should be dishonored
Because he married me before to Romeo?
I fear it is. And yet methinks it should not,
For he hath still been tried[2] a holy man.
How if, when I am laid into the tomb,
I wake before the time that Romeo
Come to redeem me? There's a fearful point.
Shall I not then be stifled in the vault,
To whose foul mouth no healthsome air breathes in,
And there die strangled ere my Romeo comes?
Or if I live, is it not very like,
The horrible conceit[3] of death and night,
Together with the terror of the place,
As in a vault, an ancient receptacle,
Where for this many hundred years the bones
Of all my buried ancestors are packed;
Where bloody Tybalt, yet but green in earth,
Lies festering in his shroud; where, as they say,
At some hours in the night spirits resort—
Alack, alack, is it not like that I
So early waking, what with loathsome smells
And shrieks like mandrakes[4] torn out of the earth,
That living mortals hearing them run mad?

---

[1] provided
[2] has always been proved
[3] idea
[4] mandragora, a narcotic root

Oh, if I wake, shall I not be distraught,
Environed with all these hideous fears,
And madly play with my forefathers' joints,
And pluck the mangled Tybalt from his shroud,
And in this rage, with some great kinsman's bone,
As with a club, dash out my desperate brains?
Oh, look! Methinks I see my cousin's ghost
Seeking out Romeo, that did spit his body
Upon a rapier's point. Stay, Tybalt, stay!
Romeo, I come! This do I drink to thee.

(She falls upon her bed, within the curtains.)

Questions

1. What do you think of the friar's advising Juliet to seemingly agree to another marriage and then fake her own death?

2. Do you think it's possible that the friar would know of such a potion as he gives Juliet? Explain.

3. As she begins this speech, Juliet is fearful. What do you think contributes to this feeling? What doubts is she having about drinking the potion?

4. If you were Juliet, how would you feel about deceiving your family? Can you think of any contemporary situations in which parents have opposed a relationship between a young couple? How was it different from this situation? How was it similar?

5. Why does Juliet have the dagger?

Playing time: One minute 30 seconds to one minute 50 seconds
Character's age: Probably 15 to 19

As You Like It

William Shakespeare/*England*

A duke has been deprived of his throne by his wicked younger brother, Frederick, and is now living in the Forest of Arden where he has established a new court.

At Duke Frederick's court, a young man named Orlando sees the banished Duke's daughter Rosalind and they fall in love. Duke Frederick exiles Rosalind and she flees with her friend Celia to join her father in the forest. There she meets Orlando.

One of the rural inhabitants is Silvius, who is in love with Phebe, a shepherdess. Not only does she not love him in return, but she asks that he deliver a letter to "Ganymede," who really is Rosalind disguised as a boy.

The following speech occurs just before Phebe asks the unsuspecting Silvius to deliver the letter. Of course, Phebe is contradicting herself throughout this monologue.

PHEBE:
> Think not I love him, though I ask for him.
> 'Tis but a peevish[1] boy, yet he talks well.
> But what care I for words? Yet words do well
> When he that speaks them pleases those that hear.
> It is a pretty youth—not very pretty—
> But, sure, he's proud, and yet his pride becomes him.
> He'll make a proper man. The best thing in him
> Is his complexion, and faster than his tongue
> Did make offense his eye did heal it up.
> He is not very tall, yet for his years he's tall.
> His leg is but soso, and yet 'tis well.
>
> There was a pretty redness in his lip,
> A little riper and more lusty red
> Than that mixed in his cheek, 'twas just the difference
> Betwixt the constant red and mingled damask.[2]
> There be some women, Silvius, had they marked him
> In parcels[3] as I did, would have gone near
> To fall in love with him. But for my part,
> I love him not nor hate him not, and yet
> I have more cause to hate him than to love him.
> For what had he to do to chide at me?
> He said mine eyes were black and my hair black,
> And, now I am remembered, scorned at me.
> I marvel why I answered not again.
> But that's all one, omittance is no quittance.[4]
> I'll write to him a very taunting letter,
> And thou shalt bear it. Wilt thou, Silvius?
> [SILVIUS: Phebe, with all my heart.]
>
> > > > > > I'll write it straight,
> The matters in my head and in my heart.
> I will be bitter with him and passing[5] short.
> Go with me, Silvius.
>
> > > > > > (Exeunt.)

---

[1] silly
[2] blended pink, the color of damask roses
[3] in parts, each separate
[4] If I let him off now, that doesn't mean he's getting off altogether
[5] exceedingly

Questions

1. Do you think it logical that Phebe doesn't suspect that "Ganymede" is really a young woman? What are the reasons that she seems to be attracted to the disguised Rosalind?

2. What kind of person is Phebe? Is she likable? Why?

3. Obviously, Phebe fell in love, or thinks she did, at first sight of "Ganymede." Is it possible to fall in love this way? Why?

4. Many of the comedies of the Elizabethan period ended with multiple marriages as does *As You Like It*. What do you think could be the reason for this?

5. Why do you think Phebe expresses such contradictory feelings about "Ganymede"?

Playing time: Seven to eight minutes
Character's age: Late teens to early 20s

Life Is a Dream

Pedro Calderón de la Barca/*Spain*

Written in 1635, this play's main plot deals with the young Prince Segismundo who is imprisoned by his father in a tower in the wilderness, the result of a soothsayer's ominous prediction. Many years later King Basilio decides to see what type of person his son is. He frees Segismundo and lets him rule. Of course, having been reared like a caged animal, the prince rules cruelly. The king has the prince drugged and returned to the tower, believing all that happened was a dream.

Later soldiers liberate Segismundo and he is restored to the throne. Now he reigns with generosity and nobility.

A subplot deals with Rosaura, the daughter of Segismundo's jailer, who restores her honor by marrying her betrayer Astolfo. In the following monologue, she appears before Segismundo to offer him her help. She feels that if he accepts it, they both will gain what they seek.

ROSAURA:

Generous Segismundo, whose heroic majesty rises from a night of
shadows into a day of deeds and dawns like the sun which, in the
arms of Aurora, returns shining to plants and roses, over mountains
and seas. Crowned with flashing rays of light, it shines forth, bathing
the hilltops with brilliance, painting the edges of the foam. So may
you, O radiant sun of Poland, dawn on the world as on this unhappy
woman, who today throws herself at your feet. Give her your aid
because she is a woman, and unfortunate: two reasons, either of
which is enough, and more than enough to obligate a man who
boasts of his chivalry. Three times have you seen me, without knowing who I am, for each time I was dressed in different clothing. At
first you thought me a man, in that rough prison where your life
made my misfortunes seem a pleasure. The second time you saw me
as a woman, when your pomp and majesty were only a dream, a
vision, a shadow. The third time is today, when, like a monstrosity of
both the sexes, I bear the weapons of a warrior, though I wear a
woman's dress. And, so that pity may the better dispose you to grant
me protection, hear, I pray, the story of my tragic fortunes. In the
Court of Muscovy I was born of a noble mother, who, since she was
unhappy, must have been very beautiful. On her a traitor cast his
eyes. I do not name him because I do not know him, and yet I know
that he was valiant; my own valor tells me this. Since I am his off-
spring, I am sorry now not to have been born a pagan, so that I
might fondly persuade myself he was a god, like one of those who in
metamorphosis rained showers of gold on Danaë, or came as swan or
bull to Leda or Europa.

I thought I was stretching out my tale too long, with these stories of
perfidy, but now I find that I have told you all in these few words:
my mother, lovelier than any woman, but unhappy as all of us, was
persuaded, alas, to love more passionately than wisely. That foolish
excuse, that promise of marriage, so carried her away that even today
she weeps to think of it. As Aeneas when he fled Troy, so this tyrant
when he fled my mother left his sword. Its blade is sheathed here,
but I will bare it before this story ends. From this imperfect knot
which neither ties nor binds, this marriage, or this crime, for it's all
one, was I then born, so like my mother that I was a portrait of her,
a true copy, not indeed of her beauty, but of her fortunes and
misfortunes. Thus I need not say that as heiress of unhappiness, I
have met a fate like hers. The most I can tell you about myself is that
the man who robbed the spoils, the trophies of my honor . . . is

Astolfo! Alas! When I name him—quite naturally, since he is my enemy—my heart fills with rage and passion. Astolfo was that ingrate, then, who forgot all our delights (since even the memory of a love that is over will fade), and came here to Poland, called from his notorious conquest, to marry Estrella, a star rising against my setting sun. Who will believe that since a star brought two lovers together, a star—Estrella—would separate them now?

I was hurt and mocked, I was crazed, grieved, and almost dead. I was indeed my ill-starred self, with all the confusion of Hell enclosed within my mind. But I kept silent, for there are pains and anxieties which the feelings express better than the tongue, and I told my trouble wordlessly until one day, when we were alone, my mother, Violante, broke open the prison of my woes. Then in troops they surged out of my breast, stumbling over one another. It did not embarrass me to tell her, for when one knows that the person in whom she confides her weaknesses has erred herself, it seems that this provides a balm and ease from pain; and thus at times a bad example has a use.

She listened sympathetically to my sorrows, and wanted to console me with her own. How easily can a judge who has sinned pardon sin in others! Having learned by her own experience that neither idleness nor lapse of time brought remedy to her lost honor, my mother decided on another course for me. Her best advice was that I follow him and compel him, by unrelenting effort, to repay his debt of honor. To accomplish this more easily, it was my fate to dress myself in man's clothing. My mother took down an ancient sword, which I now wear. Now is the time its blade should be unsheathed, as I promised her when, trusting in its sign, she said to me: "Go to Poland, and arrange for this sword you are wearing to be seen in your possession by the highest nobles. For it may be that in one of them your fortunes may find a merciful reception, and your woes some consolation."

I did arrive in Poland. Let us pass over, since it is not important, and you already know, the fact that a wild horse brought me to your cave, where you were amazed to see me. Let us pass over, too, the fact that there Clotaldo, passionately taking my part, begged the King for my life, which the King granted; that when Clotaldo learned who I was, he persuaded me to put on my own clothing and to serve Estrella. There ingeniously I obstructed Astolfo's love and marriage to Estrella. Nor do we need to mention the fact that, once more confused, you saw me here again, this time in woman's dress, and by these changes you were quite confounded. But let us come to the fact that Clotaldo, persuaded that it was important to him that Astolfo and the fair Estrella marry and rule the kingdom, advised me, against my honor, to lay aside my claim.

Therefore, since it is your turn, O valiant Segismundo, to take vengeance today—for heaven wishes you to break through the barriers of this rustic prison where your body has been a wild beast to feeling, a rock to suffering—and since your sword is lifted against your father and your country, I come to help you. On me the armor of Pallas is covered with the rich robes of Diana; I wear both cloth and steel. For both of us, then, great leader, it is important to impede and destroy these planned nuptials; for me, to keep him who is my husband from marrying another; and for you, to prevent the joining of their states, with increased power and strength, from placing our victory in doubt. As a woman, I come to persuade you to give aid to my honor, and as a man I come to encourage you to recover your crown. As a woman, I come to move you to pity when I throw myself at your feet, and as a man I come to serve you with my sword and with my person. And bear in mind that if today you court me as a woman, as a man I shall kill you in honorable defense of my honor. For I must be, in this war of love, a woman to tell you my complaints, and a man to gain honor.

Questions

1. Why do you think Rosaura would confide her past like this to Segismundo?

2. Do you feel that this scene is realistic? Why?

3. What feelings do you suppose Rosaura has as she delivers this monologue?

4. Is it logical that Rosaura speaks of herself as having the background and the abilities of both a man and a woman? Explain.

5. What is it that Rosaura wants Segismundo to do? Why?

Playing time: One minute and 50 seconds to
two minutes
Character's age: Early 20s

Le Cid

Pierre Corneille/*France*

Le Cid, written in 1636, is a tragicomedy, which means it
has both tragic and comic elements. Even though Don
Rodrigue, Le Cid, loves Chimène, he challenges her father to
a duel and kills him to avenge an insult to his own father.

Before Rodrigue can be brought to justice, he leads the
Spaniards to victory over the Moors who are attacking Seville.
He then is forced into another duel with Don Sanche, who
also loves Chimène. After Rodrigue wins, the king asks him
to postpone his marriage.

The monologue comes right at the beginning of the play
just after Chimène has asked Elvire what her father has said
in approving of her choice of husband—Rodrigue over
Sanche. She asks Elvire if she told her father that Chimène in
fact favors Rodrigue.

ELVIRE:
    No, I described your heart as indifferent,
    neither raising nor quelling the hope of either one,
    looking upon them neither severely nor with favor,
    and waiting your father's order to choose a husband.
    He loved your respect. His words and countenance
    gave instant testimony to it.
    And since you want me to repeat the story,
    this is what he said, in haste, about you and about them:
    "She is dutiful. Both men are worthy of her.
    Both come from a noble lineage that is strong and sure.
    Both young, but with eyes that reveal
    the dazzling virtue of their brave ancestors.

    Every expression on Rodrigue's face
    displays the true image of a courageous man.
    His family is so endowed with warriors
    that they seem to have been born with laurel leaves.
    The valor of his father, who was without peer in his day,
    was looked upon as miraculous.
    His prowess is now engraved in the creases of his brow,
    marking for us the sign of his past deeds.
    What the father accomplished I look for in the son,
    and if my daughter loves him, she pleases me thereby."
    He was late for the council when I saw him
    and had to cut short his speech,
    but in those few words I can tell
    he is not hesitating between your two suitors.
    The King has to choose a tutor for his son,
    and your father is the obvious choice for this honor.
    There is no doubt, for his exceptional valor
    allows no rival to be feared.
    His lofty exploits have no parallel,
    and for so well-deserved a hope there is no competition.
    Don Rodrigue has convinced his father
    to make this proposal at the end of the council.
    You may be sure he will choose the right moment,
    and all your desires will soon be realized.

Questions

1. What feelings do you think Elvire has as she reports to Chimène? Explain.

2. Why does the father favor Rodrigue over Sanche?

3. Why do you think Chimène has asked Elvire to question her father? Is this logical or believable? Explain.

4. Can you tell anything about Elvire's personality from this monologue? Explain.

5. How would you feel if one or both of your parents decided whom you should marry? How do you think Chimène would feel about this? How would Elvire feel? Explain.

The Misanthrope

Molière/ *France*

Often called the French Shakespeare, Molière is one of history's outstanding comic geniuses.

This play, written in 1666, lays bare the pretenses and failings of the French Court of Louis XIV. The central character is Alceste, who has become so bitter about the hypocrisy and superficiality of society that he wants to withdraw from the world. He is intolerant to excess of the faults that he sees in society. Yet he is in love with Célimène, very much a part of the society he despises.

Célimène enjoys baiting men with her affections and then pitting them against each other. In this scene, Arsinoé—an older lady of the court—reports to Célimène that the latter's reputation is suffering as a result of her behavior. The monologue shows Célimène's response.

CÉLIMÈNE:

Madam, I have a great many thanks to return you. Such counsel lays me under an obligation; and, far from taking it amiss, I intend this very moment to repay the favor, by giving you an advice which also touches your reputation closely; and as I see you prove yourself my friend by acquainting me with the stories that are current of me, I shall follow so nice an example, by informing you what is said of you. In a house the other day, where I paid a visit, I met some people of exemplary merit, who, while talking of the proper duties of a well spent life, turned the topic of the conversation upon you, Madam. There your prudishness and your too fervent zeal were not at all cited as a good example. This affectation of a grave demeanor, your eternal conversations on wisdom and honor, your mincings and mouthings at the slightest shadows of indecency, which an innocent though ambiguous word may convey, that lofty esteem in which you hold yourself, and those pitying glances which you cast upon all, your frequent lectures and your acrid censures on things which are pure and harmless; all this, if I may speak frankly to you, Madam, was blamed unanimously. What is the good, said they, of this modest mien and this prudent exterior, which is belied by all the rest? She says her prayers with the utmost exactness; but she beats her servants and pays them no wages. She displays great fervor in every place of devotion; but she paints and wishes to appear handsome. She covers the nudities in her pictures; but loves the reality. As for me, I undertook your defense against everyone, and positively assured them that it was nothing but scandal; but the general opinion went against me, as they came to the conclusion that you would do well to concern yourself less about the actions of others, and take a little more pains with your own; that one ought to look a long time at one's self before thinking of condemning other people; that when we wish to correct others, we ought to add the weight of a blameless life; and that even then, it would be better to leave it to those whom Heaven has ordained for the task. Madam, I also believe you to be too sensible not to take in good part this useful counsel, and not to ascribe it only to the inner promptings of an affection that feels an interest in your welfare.

Questions

1. If you met Célimène in person, how do you think you would react to her? Why?

2. Do you think you would like to play this character? Why?

3. What do you believe are Célimène's feelings as she talks to her friend? Why is she telling her what she supposedly heard about her? Do you think she actually heard all this or not? Why?

4. What do you think is the prevailing mood of this monologue? What makes you think so?

5. If you were to characterize or describe Célimène in one word, what would it be? Why?

Sixteenth and Seventeenth Centuries

Monologues
for Males

Playing time: Four minutes and 15 seconds to four minutes and 45 seconds
Character's age: Late teens

Life Is a Dream

Pedro Calderón de la Barca/*Spain*

As you learned earlier (see p. 40), Segismundo has been thrown into a tower by his father and has lived like a caged animal.

The scene from which this monologue is taken occurs near the beginning of the play. Rosaura and Clarin have just come to the tower where Segismundo is imprisoned. They don't know he is there. Just before Segismundo's speech, doors swing open and the audience sees him chained and clad in skins.

SEGISMUNDO:

Oh, wretch that I am! Oh, unfortunate! I try, oh heavens, to understand, since you treat me so, what crime I committed against you
when I was born . . . but, since I *was* born, I understand my crime.
Your cruel justice has had sufficient cause. For man's greatest crime
is to have been born at all. Still, I should like to know, to ease my
anxiety—leaving aside, ye gods, the sin of being born—in what way I
could offend you more, to deserve more punishment? Were not all
other men born too? If so, why do they have blessings that I never
enjoyed?

The bird is born, with the gaudy plumage that gives it unrivalled
beauty; and scarcely is it formed, like a flower of feathers or a winged
branch, when it swiftly cuts the vaulted air, refusing the calm shelter
of its nest. But I, with more soul, have less liberty! The beast is born,
too, with skin beautifully marked, like a cluster of stars—thanks to
Nature's skilled brush; then stern necessity, cruel and savage, teaches
it to be cruel also, and it reigns a monster in its labyrinth. Yet I, with
better instincts, have less liberty!

The fish is born, unbreathing, a creature of spawn and seaweed, and
scarcely is it seen—a scaly vessel in the waves—when it darts in all
directions, measuring the vastness of the cold and deep. And I, with
more free will, I have less liberty!

The stream is born, a snake uncoiling among the flowers, and
scarcely does this serpent of silver break through the blossoms, when
it celebrates their grace with music, and with music takes its passage
through the majesty of the open plain. Yet I, who have more life,
have less liberty!

As I reach this pitch of anger, like a volcano, an Aetna, I could tear
pieces of my heart from my own breast. What law, justice, or reason,
can deny to man so sweet a privilege, so elementary a freedom, as
God has given to a brook, a fish, a beast, and a bird?

[ROSAURA: His words make me feel pity and fear.]

SEGISMUNDO: Who's been listening to me? Clotaldo?

[CLARIN: (*Aside, to Rosaura*) Say yes!]

[ROSAURA: It's only a sad wanderer—alas!—who heard your moans in
these cold vaults.]

SEGISMUNDO: Then I shall kill you here (*He seizes her*), so that you may not know my weakness. My strong arms seize you, to tear you to pieces, only because you have heard me.

[CLARIN: I'm deaf; I couldn't hear you.]

[ROSAURA: If you were born a human being, throwing myself at your feet should be enough to make you let me go.]

SEGISMUNDO: Your voice has calmed me, your presence stopped me, and the respect I feel for you disturbs me. Who are you? For even though I know so little of the world, inasmuch as this tower has been cradle and tomb for me; and even though, since I was born—if this is to be born—I have seen only this wilderness where I live in misery, a living skeleton, a moving corpse; and even though I have seen and talked to only one man here who pities my distress, and who has taught me all I know of earth and heaven; and although here—to astonish you more, and make you call me a human monster—here among terrors and tearful fancies, I am a man among wild beasts, and a beast among men; and although in my grave misfortunes I have studied politics, been instructed by the beasts and advised by the birds, and have measured the circles of the smooth-slipping stars, you only, only you have calmed my anger, brought wonder to my eyes, and astonishment to my ears.

Each time I look at you, I feel new admiration: the more I look at you, the more I want to look. My eyes must have the dropsy, I believe, for though it's death to drink, they drink even more. And thus, although I see that seeing brings me death, I still must see. But let me look at you, and die. For if seeing you kills me, I do not know, your victim that I am, what not seeing you would do to me. It would be worse than fierce death, worse than rage, madness, and terrible grief. It would be life. And of this fate I have taken the measure, for to grant life to an unhappy man is the same as to slay a happy one.

Questions

1. What can you tell about Segismundo's feelings, his outlook on life? Explain.

2. How logical is it that Segismundo compares his life to various facets of nature? Why?

3. What is Segismundo's first reaction to hearing someone outside his cell? How does this impression change? Why?

4. Do you think it logical or believable that his father imprisoned Segismundo this way? Why or why not?

5. If possible, would you help Segismundo? Why?

▲ ▲ ▲ ▲ ▲ ▲ ▲ ▲ ▲ ▲ ▲

Playing time: Three minutes and 15 seconds to
three minutes and 45 seconds
Character's age: In his 20s

Henry V

William Shakespeare/*England*

In this play, written in 1598, King Henry tries to divert his
rebellious subjects' attention from problems at home as he
prepares to invade France. A dissolute youth, Henry has
developed into a well-intentioned king.

In this monologue, taken from Act II, scene ii, Henry
orders the execution of three English noblemen who have
accepted French gold to assassinate him.

KING HENRY:
The mercy that was quick[1] in us but late,
By your own counsel is suppressed and killed,
You must not dare, for shame, to talk of mercy,
For your own reasons[2] turn into your bosoms,
As dogs upon their masters, worrying you.
See you, my Princes and my noble peers,
These English monsters! My Lord of Cambridge here,
You know how apt our love was to accord
To furnish him with all appertinents
Belonging to his honor. And this man
Hath, for a few light crowns, lightly conspired,
And sworn unto the practice[3] of France,
To kill us here in Hampton. To the which
This knight, no less for bounty bound to us
Than Cambridge is, hath likewise sworn. But, oh,
What shall I say to thee, Lord Scroop? Thou cruel,
Ingrateful, savage, and inhuman creature!
Thou that didst bear the key of all my counsels,
That knew'st the very bottom of my soul,
That almost mightst have coined me into gold
Wouldst thou have practiced on me for thy use,
May it be possible that foreign hire
Could out of thee extract one spark of evil
That might annoy[4] my finger? 'Tis so strange
That, though the truth of it stands off as gross[5]
As black and white, my eye will scarcely see it.
Treason[6] and murder ever kept together,
As two yoke devils sworn to either's purpose,
Working so grossly in a natural cause
That admiration[7] did not hoop[8] at them.
But thou, 'gainst all proportion, didst bring in
Wonder to wait on treason and on murder.

---

[1] living
[2] arguments
[3] plots
[4] hurt
[5] obvious
[6] Most often treason and murder work together and have some excuse for their actions, which seems so natural that no one is surprised.
[7] wonder
[8] cry out

And whatsoever cunning fiend it was
That wrought upon thee so preposterously
Hath got the voice[9] in Hell for excellence.
All other devils that suggest by treasons
Do botch and bungle up damnation
With patches, colors, and with forms being fetched
From glistering[10] semblances of piety.
But he that tempered[11] thee bade thee stand up,[12]
Gave thee no instance[13] why thou shouldst do treason,
Unless to dub[14] thee with the name of traitor.
If that same demon that hath gulled[15] thee thus
Should with his lion gait[16] walk the whole world,
He might return to vasty Tartar[17] back,
And tell the legions "I can never win
A soul so easy as that Englishman's."
Oh, how hast thou with jealousy infected
The sweetness of affiance![18] Show men dutiful?
Why, so didst thou. Seem they grave and learned?
Why, so didst thou. Come they of noble family?
Why, so didst thou. Seem they religious?
Why, so didst thou. Or are they spare in diet,
Free from gross passion or of mirth or anger,
Constant in spirit, not swerving with the blood,[19]
Garnished and decked in modest complement,[20]
Not working with the eye without the ear,
And but in purged[21] judgment trusting neither?
Such and so finely bolted[22] didst thou seem.
And thus thy fall hath left a kind of blot,
To mark the full-fraught[23] man and best indued[24]

---

[9] vote
[10] falsely glittering
[11] molded
[12] stand up as a finished work of art
[13] reason
[14] confer the title of knight upon
[15] cheated
[16] lion's walk
[17] hell
[18] trust or loyalty
[19] passion or lust
[20] outward signs of a noble man
[21] free from bias
[22] sifted as fine flower
[23] fully laden
[24] endowed

With some suspicion. I will weep for thee,
For this revolt of thine, methinks, is like
Another fall of man. Their faults are open,
Arrest them to the answer of the law,
And God acquit them of their practices!

Questions

1. From this monologue, what can you tell about the sort of person King Henry V is? Explain.

2. What emotions do you think Henry is feeling here? How do you know?

3. How does Henry feel about the men he is condemning? Explain.

4. Do you believe Henry should have the three men executed? Why?

5. How do you think you would feel in Henry's place? Would you react differently to the treason of the three men? Why?

Playing time: Four minutes to four minutes and 30 seconds
Character's age: Early 20s

Volpone

Ben Jonson/*England*

The play is a comedy satirizing greed and the lust for life. Volpone, with the help of Mosca, described in the cast of characters as his parasite, feigns fatal illness and so tricks Boltore, Corbaccio, and Corvino into promising him their wealth in the hope of inheriting Volpone's estates and fortune. Corvino even pledges Celia, his wife. Celia and Bonario, Corbaccio's son, innocent victims, are finally saved when Mosca and Volpone overreach themselves so far that they expose themselves to the justice of a Venetian court.

In this scene, Volpone is talking to Celia about Corvino's pledging her to him. He tries to overwhelm her by telling all the feelings she inspires in him and how he feels about her.

VOLPONE:

Ay, in Corvino, and such earth-fed minds, (*leaping from his couch*)
That never tasted the true heaven of love.
Assure thee, Celia, he that would sell thee,
Only for hope of gain, and that uncertain,
He would have sold his part of Paradise
For ready money, had he met a cope-man.[1]
Why art thou mazed to see me thus revived?
Rather applaud thy beauty's miracle;

'Tis thy great work: that hath, not now alone.
But sundry times raised me, in several shapes,
And, but this morning, like a mountebank,
To see thee at thy window: ay, before
I would have left my practice, for thy love.
In varying figures, I would have contended
With the blue Proteus, or the horned flood.
Now art thou welcome.

[CELIA: Sir!]

VOLPONE: Nay, fly me not.

Nor let thy false imagination
That I was bed-rid, make thee think I am so:
Thou shalt not find it. I am now as fresh,
As hot, as high, and in as jovial plight
As, when, in that so celebrated scene,
At recitation of our comedy,
For entertainment of the great Valois,
I acted young Antinous; and attracted
The eyes and ears of all the ladies present.
To admire each graceful gesture, note, and footing.
(*Sings*)

Come, my Celia, let us prove
While we can, the sports of love,
Time will not be ours forever,
He, at length, our good will sever;
Spend not then his gifts in vain:
Suns that set may rise again;
But if once we lose this light,
'Tis with us perpetual night.
Why should we defer our joys?

---

[1] merchant

Fame and rumor are but toys.
Cannot we delude the eyes
Of a few poor household spies?
Or his easier ears beguile,
Thus removed by our wile?
'Tis no sin love's fruits to steal;
But the sweet thefts to reveal:
To be taken, to be seen,
These have crimes accounted been.

[CELIA: Some serene blast me, or dire lightning strike
This my offending face!]

VOLPONE: Why droops my Celia?
Thou hast, in the place of a base husband found
A worthy lover: use thy fortune well,
With secrecy and pleasure. See, behold,
What thou art queen of; not in expectation,
As I feed others: but processed and crowned.
See, here, a rope of pearl; and each more orient
Than the brave Ægyptian queen caroused:
Dissolve and drink them. See, a carbuncle,
May put out both the eyes of our St. Mark;
A diamond would have bought Lollia Paulina,
When she came in like star-light, hid with jewels,
That were the spoils of provinces, take these
And wear, and lose them; yet remains an earring
To purchase them again, and this whole state.
A gem but worth a private patrimony,
In nothing; we will eat such at a meal.
The heads of parrots, tongues of nightingales,
The brains of peacocks, and of estriches,[2]
Shall be our food, and, could we get the phoenix,
Though nature lost her kind, she were our dish.

[CELIA: Good sir, these things might move a mind affected
With such delights; but I, whose innocence
Is all I can think wealthy, or worth th' enjoying,
And which, once lost, I have nought to lose beyond it,
Cannot be taken with these sensual baits:
If you have conscience——]

---

[2] ostriches

VOLPONE: 'Tis the beggar's virtue;
  If thou hast wisdom, hear me, Celia.
  Thy baths shall be the juice of July-flowers,
  Spirit of roses, and of violets.
  The milk of unicorns, and panthers' breath
  Gathered in bags, and mixed with Cretan wines.
  Our drink shall be prepared gold and amber;
  Which we will take until my roof whirl round
  With the vertigo: and my dwarf shall dance,
  My eunuch sing, my fool make up the antic,
  Whilst we, in changed shapes, act Ovid's tales,
  Thou, like Europa now, and I like Jove,
  Then I like Mars, and thou like Erycine:
  So of the rest, till we have quite run through,
  And wearied all the fables of the gods.
  Then will I have thee in more modern forms,
  Attired like some sprightly dame of France,
  Brave Tuscan lady, or proud Spanish beauty;
  Sometimes unto the Persian sophy's[3] wife;
  Or the grand signior's mistress; and for change,
  To one of our most artful courtezans,
  Or some quick Negro, or cold Russian;
  And I will meet thee in as many shapes:
  Where we may so transfuse our wandering souls
  Out at our lips, and score up sums of pleasures,
  (*Sings*)
    That the curious shall not know
    How to tell them as they flow;
    And the envious, when they find
    What their number is, be pined.

Questions

1. How do you think Volpone feels about Celia? Of course, he is
   trying to flatter her, but is he being sincere?

2. Why does Celia find what Volpone says insulting?

---

[3] Persian ruler

3. If you heard a person today saying things like this (of course, in modern terms) to a girl or woman, what would be your reaction? Why?

4. Why do you suppose Volpone begins singing to Celia?

5. Do you think this is a good monologue to perform? Why?

Playing time: Two minutes and 5 seconds to two minutes and 25 seconds
Character's age: 18 to 20

Phaedra

Jean Racine/*France*

P haedra, who is married to Theseus and who is descended of gods and monsters, is the victim of Aphrodite's hate. The goddess has caused her to feel a guilty passion for her stepson Hippolytus. When it is reported wrongly that Theseus is dead, Phaedra's confidante Oenone argues that Phaedra's passion could no longer be considered adulterous.

Phaedra confesses her love to Hippolytus, who is shocked and disgusted. He is in love with Aricia, a captive princess. As a result, when Theseus returns, Phaedra lets Oenone accuse Hippolytus of her own crime.

Theseus invokes Poseidon to punish Hippolytus, who slays the young man. When Phaedra learns what has happened, she takes poison. Dying at Theseus' feet, she confesses what she has done.

This play, of course, is based on the same myth as the Greek play *Hippolytus*. As you can see, there are a number of variations.

In this scene, which occurs near the beginning of Racine's play (*Phèdre*, in French), Hippolytus is explaining to his tutor Theramenes why he wants to leave Troezen. The tutor at first thinks he wants to flee from Phaedra, but Hippolytus says that it is Aricia he wants to leave. Theramenes asks him why he "hates" Aricia; he says he doesn't hate her. In this monologue he explains what he means.

HIPPOLYTUS:

My friend, you must not ask me.
You, who have known my heart through all my life,
And know it to be proud and most disdainful,—
You will not ask that I should shame myself
By now disowning all that I professed.
My mother was an Amazon,—my wildness,
Which you think strange, I suckled at her breast,
And as I grew, why, Reason did approve
What Nature planted in me. Then you told me
The story of my father, and you know
How, often, when I listened to your voice
I kindled, hearing of his noble acts,—
And you would tell how he brought consolation
To mortals, for the absence of Alcides,
And how he cleared the roads of monsters,—robbers,—
Procrustes, Cercyron, Sciro, Sinnis slain,
Scattered the Epidaurian giant's bones,
And how Crete ran with blood of the Minotaur![1]
But when you told me of less glorious deeds,—
Troth plighted here and there and everywhere,
Young Helen stolen from her home at Sparta,
And Peribœa's tears in Salamis,
And many other trusting ones deceived,
Whose very names he cannot now remember,—
Lone Ariadne, crying to the rocks,—
And last of all this Phædra, bound to him
By better ties,—You know that with regret
I heard, and urged that you cut short the tale.
I had been happier, could I erase
This one unworthy part of his bright story
Out of my memory. Must I in turn
Be made love's slave, and brought to bend so low?
It is the more contemptible in me,
For no such brilliance clings about my name
As to the name of Theseus,—no monsters quelled
Have given me the right to share his weakness.
And if I must be humbled for my pride,
Aricia should have been the last to tame me!

---

[1] Theseus destroyed the Cretan bull, the monster Minotaur who each year devoured seven young men and women whom Athens sent to Crete as a tribute.

Was I not mad that I should have forgotten
Those barriers which must keep us far apart
Eternally? For by my father's order
Her brothers' blood must never flow again
In a child of hers. He dreads a single shoot
From any stock so guilty, and would bury
Their name with her; so even to the tomb
No torch of Hymen[2] may be lit for her.
Shall I espouse her rights against my father,
Provoke his wrath, launch on a mad career?—

Questions

1. Why does Hippolytus want to flee from Aricia? Do you think this is a good reason? Why?

2. What is the prevailing mood in this scene? How, as an actor, can you try to communicate this to an audience?

3. If you were Hippolytus' tutor, how would you react to what he says? Explain.

4. What can you tell about Hippolytus' personality from this scene? Is he believable? Why?

5. Do you think Hippolytus' reasons for wanting to leave Aricia are logical? Do you think a person in the present would consider these sorts of things if he fell in love?

---

[2] The god of marriage, symbolized by burning torches.

Playing time: Three minutes and 20 seconds to three minutes and 50 seconds
Character's age: Probably his early 20s

Le Cid

Pierre Corneille/*France*

This monologue is taken from Act IV, scene iii, where Rodrigue, whom you remember is the man Chimène loves (see p. 44), is recounting his victory in leading the Spaniards against the Moors who were attacking Seville.

The play revolves around the theme of love versus honor. Rodrigue and Chimène are forced to choose between love for each other and duty to their parents. The play caused a great deal of controversy. One of the reasons is Chimène's apparently agreeing to marry Rodrigue who had killed her father less than twenty-four hours earlier.

RODRIGUE:
Under my direction these men advanced.
And showed on their faces a virile confidence.
We were five hundred at first, but with a swift reinforcement,
we were three thousand when we reached the harbor;
and seeing us march, with determination in our faces,
the most terrified recovered their courage.
On arriving, I hid two-thirds of the men
in the bottom of the boats which we found there.
The rest, whose numbers increased hourly,
remained close by, devoured by impatience,
and lay on the ground, where they kept silence,
and spent a part of a magnificent night.
At my command, the guard did likewise,
and staying out of sight, they helped my stratagem.
Then I boldly pretended I had received from you
the order I announced and gave to all.
That obscure light which falls from the stars
at last showed us, with the tide, thirty ships.
The wave swelled under them, and in a joint effort
the Moors and the sea entered the harbor.
We let them pass. Everything seemed quiet to them.
Not a soldier at the harbor, not a soldier at the city walls.
Our deep silence deceived them
and they no longer doubted they had caught us.
Fearlessly they approached, anchored, disembarked,
and rushed into the hands waiting for them.
We rose up then, and all together
uttered a thousand war cries which reached the heavens.
More of our men answered these cries from their ships.
We appeared in arms. The Moors were thrown into rout.
Terror seized them while they were still landing.
Before the fighting began, they knew they had lost.
They were bent on pillaging and they encountered battle.
We attacked by water and by land,
and caused rivers of their blood to flow
before one of them could resist.
But soon, in spite of us, their princes rallied them,
their courage came back and their terror fled.
The shame of dying without combat
stopped their confusion and reanimated their valor.

Against us they firmly drew their scimitars
and made a horrible mingling of our blood with theirs.
The land, the river, their ships, the harbor
were the sites of slaughter where death reigned.
　　Countless acts and courageous deeds
were not even visible under the cover of darkness,
where each man, the only witness of his own thrusts,
could not see whom fortune was favoring.
I went everywhere encouraging our men,
making some move ahead, lending support to others,
placing those who joined with us, urging them on,
and I did not know the result until daybreak.
At last its light showed our advantage.
The Moors saw their defeat and then lost courage
when they saw reinforcements come to our help.
The hope of victory turned into the fear of death.
They reached their ships and cut the cables.
With terrible shrieks resounding everywhere,
they retreated in an uproar, without considering
whether their kings could retreat with them.
Their terror was too strong for them to heed this duty.
The incoming tide had brought them, and the ebb tide took them
　　away
while their kings, in combat with us,
and a few of their men, wounded by our swords,
fought valiantly and sold their lives dearly.
In vain I urged them to surrender,
but they held their scimitars and refused to listen.
Then seeing all their men fall at their feet
and aware they were fighting in vain,
they asked for the leader. I came forward and they surrendered.
I sent both of them to you at the same time.
And the fighting stopped because there were no more fighters.

Questions

1. In your own words, describe the battle that Le Cid recounts for the king.

2. How do you think Le Cid feels about what has happened? Point to specific lines that support your views.

3. What can you tell about Rodrigue's personality from this mono-logue? Do you think he's a good soldier or leader?

4. From the monologue, what can you discover that contributed to the Spanish victory?

5. Do you think you'd like to have a man like Le Cid for a friend? Why?

Playing time: Two minutes and 15 seconds to
two minutes and 35 seconds
Character's age: Early 20s

The Miser

Molière/*France*

Harpagon, a widower and the father of a grown son and
daughter, allows his miserliness to dictate his every action,
frustrating his children and making him the target of all who
recognize his all-consuming obsession.

His children scheme to choose their own mates rather than
those chosen by their father who would gain financially from
the liaisons.

In this scene, the son Cléante, who becomes his father's
rival for the affections of Mariane, describes his feelings about
her to his sister. Cléante doesn't yet know that his father
wants to marry the same girl.

CLÉANTE:

A young girl who has been living nearby for a short time, and who seems created to inspire love in all who see her. Nature has fashioned nothing more lovable. I felt enthralled from the moment I saw her. Her name is Mariane and she lives under the protection of her mother, a good woman who is nearly always ill, and for whom this dear girl shows the greatest kindness imaginable. She waits upon her, sympathizes with her, and consoles her with a tenderness that would touch your soul. She has the most charming way in the world in whatever she does, and her every action shines with a thousand graces. Such attractive gentleness, such engaging goodness, such adorable modesty, such—Ah! Élise, if you could only see her.

[ÉLISE: I see a great deal of her, Cléante, in what you tell me. And to understand what she is, it is enough for me that you love her.]

CLÉANTE: I have found out, secretly, that they are not very well off, and that, even though they live frugally, they have a difficult time making ends meet. Imagine, Élise, what joy it would be to be able to raise the fortune of the person one loves, discreetly to give some slight help to the modest needs of a virtuous family. Just think how miserable it makes me to find myself powerless, because of my father's avarice, to taste that pleasure, or to show the dear girl any evidence of my love.

[ÉLISE: Yes, Cléante, I can see how grieved you must be.]

CLÉANTE: Ah! Élise, far more than you can imagine. Have you ever seen anything more cruel than this rigorous economy exercised over us, than this unheard-of-stinginess we are made to languish under? What good will wealth do us, if it comes only when we are no longer young enough to enjoy it; if even to maintain myself, I am forced on every side to run into debt; if you and I are reduced to obtaining daily help from tradesmen to keep decent clothes on our back? So, I have wanted to talk with you, to ask you to help me sound father out about my present feelings. If he disapproves, I am resolved to go away with this dear girl, and enjoy whatever fortune Heaven may offer us. I am trying now to obtain money everywhere for this purpose; and if your difficulties resemble mine, Élise, if father insists on opposing our desires, we shall both leave him and free ourselves from the tyranny his unbearable avarice has so long imposed on us.

Questions

1. What do you think of Cléante's plans to help Mariane and her mother? In light of his situation, is this a realistic goal? Why?

2. Cléante says that if his father opposes his sister's and his desires, they should leave. What do you think about that decision?

3. Do you sympathize with Cléante? Why?

4. What would you do in a situation like this—where you were in love with someone but had no money to marry and had to rely on your father's approval?

5. If you were playing this role, what feelings would you try to communicate to your audience? Why?

Monologues
for Females

Playing time: Two minutes to two minutes and
20 seconds
Character's age: Early 20s

The Rivals

Richard Brinsley Sheridan/*Ireland*

This play is a comedy in which there is a lot of confusion
over identity. The main plot deals with Lydia Languish, a
sentimental heroine whose fortune depends on the whims of
her aunt, Mrs. Malaprop.

One of the subplots involves Faulkland and Julia, a pair of
sentimental lovers. In this scene from Act V, Faulkland has
told Julia that he must flee England because of a crime he
committed. He tells her this only to test her love, which never
really was in doubt.

When she says she'll flee with him, he finally believes that
she really does love him. He tries to kiss her, but she fends him
off and delivers this monologue.

JULIA:

Hold, Faulkland!—That you are free from a crime, which I before feared to name, Heaven knows how sincerely I rejoice! These are tears of thankfulness for that! But that your cruel doubts should have urged you to an imposition that has wrung my heart, gives me now a pang more keen than I can express . . .

Yet, hear me,—My father loved you, Faulkland, and you preserved the life that tender parent gave me; in his presence I pledged my hand—joyfully pledged it—where before I had given my heart. When, soon after, I lost that parent, it seemed to me that Providence had, in Faulkland, shown me whither to transfer without a pause, my grateful duty, as well as my affection; hence I have been content to bear from you what pride and delicacy would have forbid me from another. I will not upbraid you, by repeating how you have trifled with my sincerity . . .

After such a year of trial, I might have flattered myself that I should not have been insulted with a new probation of my sincerity, as cruel as unnecessary! I now see it is not in your nature to be content or confident in love. With this conviction—I never will be yours. While I had hopes that my persevering attention, and unreproaching kindness, might in time reform your temper, I should have been happy to have gained a dearer influence over you; but I will not furnish you with a licensed power to keep alive an incorrigible fault, at the expense of one who never would contend with you . . .

But one word more.—As my faith has once been given to you, I never will barter it with another.—I shall pray for your happiness with the truest sincerity; and the dearest blessing I can ask of Heaven to send you will be to charm you from that unhappy temper, which alone has prevented the performance of our solemn engagement. All I request of you is that you will yourself reflect upon this infirmity, and when you number up the many true delights it has deprived you of, let it not be your least regret, that it lost you the love of one who would have followed you in beggary through the world!

Questions

1. What do you think of Faulkland's telling Julia of a crime he really didn't commit?

2. Julia says that now she is leaving Faulkland. What are her reasons? Do you think she should leave him? Why?

3. What is the mood of this scene? Explain. How would you convey it to an audience?

4. What sort of emotions is Julia feeling? Why?

5. What sort of person is Julia? Why do you think so?

Playing time: One minute and 50 seconds to two minutes and 10 seconds
Character's age: 18 to 19

The Contrast

Royall Tyler/ *U.S.A.*

In this early American comedy, Dimple has returned from Europe with a lot of debts, European affectations, and a scorn of all things American. He plans to break off his contracted match with Maria and marry a rich woman, Letitia.

In this monologue from Act I, Maria does not yet know that her marriage to Dimple will never take place.

MARIA:

(*Alone*.) How deplorable is my situation! How distressing for a daughter to find her heart militating with her filial duty! I know my father loves me tenderly. Why then do I reluctantly obey him? Heaven knows! with what reluctance I should oppose the will of a parent, or set an example of filial disobedience; at a parent's command I could wed awkwardness and deformity.

Were the heart of my husband good, I would so magnify his good qualities with the eye of conjugal affection, that the defects of his person and manners should be lost in the emanation of his virtues. At a father's command, I could embrace poverty. Were the poor man my husband, I would learn resignation to my lot; I would enliven our frugal meal with good humour, and chase away misfortune from our cottage with a smile. At a father's command, I could almost submit, to what every female heart knows to be the most mortifying, to marry a weak man, and blush at my husband's folly in every company I visited.—But to marry a depraved wretch, whose only virtue is a polished exterior; who is actuated by the unmanly ambition of conquering the defenseless; whose heart, insensible to the emotions of partriotism, dilates at the plaudits of every unthinking girl: whose laurels are the sighs and tears of the miserable victims of his specious behaviour.—Can he, who has no regard for the peace and happiness of other families, ever have a due regard for the peace and happiness of his own? Would to heaven that my father were not so hasty in his temper! Surely, if I were to state my reasons for declining this match, he would not compel me to marry a man— whom, though my lips may solemnly promise to honour, I find my heart must ever despise.   (*Exit.*)

Questions

1. How would you describe Maria? What type of person is she?

2. How would you describe her feelings in this monologue? Explain.

3. Do you agree with how she says she would treat a husband, no matter who he is? Why?

4. The play is a comedy. Do you find this monologue funny or amusing? Why?

5. Would you play Maria in a realistic or exaggerated manner? Why?

Playing time: One minute and 40 seconds to one minute and 50 seconds
Character's age: 18 to 20

The Sea Gull

Anton Chekhov/*Russia*

Among those gathered at the Sorin estate are Madame Terpleff, a selfish, middle-aged actress and her lover Trigorin, a popular writer. Her son Konstantine wants to be a good writer but isn't, and he wants to marry Nina, daughter of a nearby landowner and an aspiring actress.

In a fit of jealousy, Konstantine shoots a sea gull and lays it at Nina's feet. Trigorin uses this image in a story, and Nina sees herself as a sea gull.

She has run off with Trigorin, who later deserts her. She discovers that she cannot be a great actress but works in touring shows.

It is two years later, and Nina has been through a lot of hardship, including the death of her baby. In the following monologue, Nina is talking to Konstantine. Later, after this second rejection by Nina, Konstantine commits suicide.

NINA:

Why do you say you kiss the ground I walk on? I ought to be killed. (*Bends over desk*) I'm so tired. If I could rest . . . rest. I'm a sea gull. No, that's not it. I'm an actress. Well, no matter. . . . (*Hears Arkadina and Trigorin laughing in the dining room. She listens, runs to the door on the left and peeps through the keyhole*) and he's here too. (*Goes to Trepleff*) Well, no matter. He didn't believe in the theatre, all my dreams he'd laugh at, and little by little I quit believing in it myself, and lost heart. And there was the strain of love, jealousy, constant anxiety about my little baby. I got to be small and trashy, and played without thinking. I didn't know what to do with my hands, couldn't stand properly on the stage, couldn't control my voice. You can't imagine the feeling when you are acting and know it's dull. I'm a sea gull. No, that's not it. Do you remember, you shot a sea gull? A man comes by chance, sees it, and out of nothing else to do, destroys it. That's not it. . . . (*Puts her hand to her forehead*) What was I . . . I was talking about the stage. Now I'm not like that. I'm a real actress, I act with delight, with rapture, I'm drunk when I'm on the stage, and feel that I am beautiful. And now, ever since I've been here, I've kept walking about, kept walking and thinking, thinking and believing my soul grows stronger every day. Now I know, I understand, Kostya, that in our work . . . acting or writing . . . what matters is not fame, not glory, not what I used to dream about, it's how to endure, to bear my cross, and have faith. I have faith and it all doesn't hurt me so much, and when I think of my calling I'm not afraid of life.

Questions

1. Describe the symbolism attached to the sea gull.

2. How would you describe Nina? What sort of person is she?

3. Why do you think Nina keeps losing the thread of what she's saying? Do you feel sorry for her? Why?

4. What feelings is Nina experiencing in this scene? What is the prevailing mood?

5. Can you empathize with Nina? Explain.

The Importance of Being Earnest

Oscar Wilde/*Ireland*

This is a very witty and satirical comedy in which two young men seek the hands of two young ladies, despite social obstacles. Another obstacle is that the two women feel that they cannot marry anyone who is not named Ernest.

The men are Jack and Algernon, the women Gwendolen and Cecily. The latter is Jack's ward.

The monologue occurs about three-fourths of the way through the second of three acts and takes place at Jack's country estate. Gwendolen, who is in love with Jack, has just discovered that Cecily is his ward. This makes her immediately jealous.

GWENDOLEN:

Oh! It is strange he never mentioned to me that he had a ward. How secretive of him! He grows more interesting hourly. I am not sure, however, that the news inspires me with feelings of unmixed delight. (*Rising and going to her.*) I am very fond of you, Cecily: I have liked you ever since I met you! But I am bound to state that now that I know that you are Mr. Worthing's ward, I cannot help expressing a wish you were—well, just a little older than you seem to be—and not quite so very alluring in appearance. In fact, if I may speak candidly—

[CECILY: Pray do! I think that whenever one has anything unpleasant to say, one should always be quite candid.]

GWENDOLEN: Well, to speak with perfect candor, Cecily, I wish that you were fully forty-two, and more than usually plain for your age. Ernest has a strong upright nature. He is the very soul of truth and honour. Disloyalty would be as impossible to him as deception. But even men of the noblest possible moral character are extremely susceptible to the influence of the physical charms of others. Modern, no less than Ancient History, supplies us with many most painful examples of what I refer to. If it were not so, indeed, History would be quite unreadable.

Questions

1. Why does Gwendolen say she wishes Cecily were older and plain?

2. What provides the humor in this scene? Explain.

3. Why does Gwendolen talk about Ernest's (really Jack's) character?

4. What can you tell about Gwendolen's character from what she says?

5. Would you like playing this role? Why?

Monologues
for Males

Peer Gynt

Hernani

Secret Service

Peer Gynt

Henrik Ibsen/*Norway*

Peer Gynt is fantasy and satire, written in verse. The title character, who comes from folklore, is an unprincipled rogue who wastes his life doing pretty much as he likes, through evasion and compromise. At the beginning of the play he kidnaps a young bride from her wedding feast in vengeance for another young woman's slight. This second woman, Solveig, follows him to the mountains and warns him that the people from the village are after him.

In the meantime the villagers avenge themselves on Peer's aged mother by taking everything but her bed. Peer deserts Solveig to escape the villagers and sneaks back to his dying mother's side, comforting her and regaling her with fantastic stories. Then he flees Norway.

This scene occurs at the beginning of Act III, where Peer is in the mountains building a dwelling.

PEER GYNT:
>Oh yes, you're tough, my dear old friend!
>But it won't avail you; your days are numbered.
>>(*Starts hacking again*)
>I know you're wearing a coat of mail,[1]
>But I'll pierce it through, strong as it is.
>Oh yes, you can shake your twisted arms;
>You're resentful and angry, I understand.
>But I'm going to make you fall to your knees—!
>>(*Breaks off suddenly*)
>More lies! This is no hero in armor;
>More lies! It's nothing but an old tree,
>Only a fir with its bark all cracked.
>It's heavy work, this timber-felling,
>But it's worse when you muddle it up with daydreams.
>They must stop, these wonderful cloudy flights
>To an airy world that never was.
>You're an outlaw, my lad, a forest outlaw.
>>(*Hacks away for a time in a great hurry*)
>Yes, a fugitive! You've no mother now
>To lay your table and bring you your food.
>If you want to eat you must help yourself,
>Hunt in the forest and fish in the streams,
>Chop your own wood and light your own fire,
>Build your own house and set it in order.
>You want warm clothes? You must kill a reindeer.
>You want your own house? You must break the stones.
>You want oak beams? You must saw the wood
>And carry it home on your own broad back.
>>(*Lowers his axe and stares straight in front of him*)
>I'll build myself a thing of beauty,
>With a tower and a weather-vane;
>and on the gable-end I will carve
>A mermaid with a long swishing tail.
>The weather-vane and the locks will be
>Embossed with brass. I might get some glass
>For the windows: and strangers far off will gape
>And wonder at the glory of it.
>>(*Laughing uncomfortably*)

---

[1] armor

Romancing and lies! I'm at it again.
You're an outlaw!
(*Starts working again with a new relish*)

A hut with a decent roof
Will keep out the rain as well as the frost.
(*Looks up at the tree*)
He's beginning to totter. One more blow!
He's fallen! He's prostrate at my feet.
The young trees are trembling all around.
(*Begins to lop off the branches; suddenly, he stops and listens, his axe upraised*)
There's someone after me! Can it be
The old man from Heggstad trying his tricks?
(*Crouches behind a tree and peeps out cautiously*)
A boy! Just a lad! He seems afraid;
So furtive, too. What's that he's hidden
Under his jacket? A sickle? He's peering
All round him. He's putting his hand on a branch.
What's he doing now? He's so still, so tense. . . .
Oh, horrible! He's chopped his finger off!
Right off! And he's bleeding like an ox.
He's running off with a rag round his hand.
(*Goes nearer*)
This is the very Devil! A finger!
Right off! And he did it deliberately.
Aha! Now I see! It's a certain way
Of keeping out of the King's Service.
That must be it! They wanted him to fight
And he had his own ideas about war.
But to chop it off—! To maim himself—!
Think about it, yes; have the wish, the intention.
But do it! No! That is beyond me.
(*He shakes his head, then carries on with his work*)

Questions

1. What can you tell about Peer's feelings in this scene?

2. Why do you think Peer addresses the tree as a friend?

3. Can you tell anything about the type of person Peer is just from this scene?

4. Why do you suppose Peer talks about the young man who cuts off his finger? What do you think was Ibsen's purpose in including this part?

5. What do you think Peer's attitude is about being an outlaw?

Playing time: Four minutes and 20 seconds to four minutes and 50 seconds
Character's age: Early 20s

Hernani

Victor Hugo/*France*

Set in 1519 in Spain, the play is about Hernani, a nobleman who is rebelling against King Charles who has been the cause of his father's death. Hernani loves Doña Sol, who is to marry her uncle, Don Ruy.

The play is important because it changed the French rules of drama and caused a debate that ranged for forty-five nights. The argument over what should constitute drama so interrupted the performances that it was nearly impossible to hear the actors.

The play is a combination of genres, which had not been allowed in the French theatre to this point. It's romantic melodrama, except that it ends in the deaths of Doña Sol and Hernani.

In this scene, Hernani tells Doña Sol that he is not worthy of her love.

HERNANI:

I have blasphemed! Doña Sol, if I were in your stead, I should have
had enough; I should be weary of this wild fool, of this brooding,
senseless man who knows not how to kiss till he has wounded. I
should tell him "Go." Turn me away, you must! And I shall only
bless you, for you were good, and kind; for you have borne me far
too long already, for I am evil, I would darken your days with my
black nights.

It is too much—your spirit is high and good and pure: if I am bad,
why should you suffer for it? Wed the old duke, he is a good man,
and noble; he owns Olmedo from his mother, Alcala from his father.
Once more I bid you, be rich with him: be happy! Do you know
what splendid gifts my own generous hand can offer you? A dowry of
sorrow. A choice between blood and tears. Exile, chains, death, the
constant fear around me—there is your golden necklace, and your
handsome crown, and never has proud husband offered his bride a
richer treasure chest of pain and mourning! Marry the old man, I tell
you. He deserves you. Who would ever match my doomed head with
your clear brow? Who ever, seeing the two of us—you calm and fair,
me violent and perilous, you tranquil and blossoming like a shaded
flower, me storm-tossed against a thousand different reefs—who
would think to say our fates are joined by a single law? No. God,
who determines good things, did not make you for me. I have no
heaven-sent right to you. I am resigned. I have your heart, but I
have it by theft. I hand it to another, worthier man. Heaven has
never consented to our love. When I told you it was your destiny, I
lied. And in any case, farewell to all revenge and love! My day is
done. I'll go then, futile, with my double dream, unable either to
win love or to punish. I should have been built to hate, but I can
only love! Forgive me, and flee! These prayers are all I ask: do not
refuse them, for they are my last. You live, and I am dead. You must
not wall yourself into my tomb with me.

[DOÑA SOL: Ungrateful love!]

HERNANI: Mountains of Aragon! Galicia, Estremadura! I bring misfortune to all who join with me. I have taken your best sons to serve my
claims; relentless, I have sent them into battle, and they are dead of
it. They were the most valiant in all of valiant Spain. And they are
dead. They have fallen in the mountains, all of them upon their
backs as brave men do, before God: if they were to open their eyes
again, they would see the blue heavens. And this is what I do to all

who join me. Is this a destiny that you should want to share? Doña Sol, take the duke—take hell itself, take the king! Anyone is better! There is not one friend left who thinks of me; everything else gone, and now your turn has come to leave me too, for I must live alone. Flee my contamination; do not make a religion of love. Oh, have mercy on yourself, and flee! . . . Perhaps you think me a man like all the rest, a rational thing who first perceives his goal and then will move straight toward it. Do not be fooled— I am not such a man. I am a resistless energy— the blind and deafened agent of doleful mysteries, a soul of sorrows bound together with darkness. Where am I bound? I cannot say. But yet I feel myself hurled on by some impulsive gale, some wild determination. I fall, and fall, and never do I rest. . . . If once, gasping for breath, I dare to turn my head, a voice commands "Go on!"; and the chasm is a deep one, and the depth of it is red with blood or flame! And meanwhile, along my headlong course, all things are crushed, or die. Woe to him who comes close to me! Oh, flee! Turn from my fated path. Against my will I'll do you injury!

Questions

1. What do you think is Hernani's mood in this monologue? Explain.

2. *Hernani* is a melodrama, which means, among other things, that it is exaggerated. Can you find any exaggeration in this scene? Explain.

3. Why do you think Hernani is so willing to give up Doña Sol to another man?

4. If you were playing this role, what mood would you try to communicate to an audience?

5. Do you think Hernani is a believable character? Explain.

Playing time: Fifty seconds to one minute and
10 seconds
Character's age: 16

Secret Service

William Gillette/ *U.S.A.*

At the beginning of this melodrama, the Union Army is threatening Richmond. Two brothers, members of the secret service, are to seize control of the telegraph office and send false orders to the commander of the Confederate Army, thus allowing Union forces to capture Richmond.

In this scene, Wilfred wants to be allowed to join his father in fighting against the Union Army. His mother doesn't want to let him go because he's only sixteen. Yet he argues that in a day or two young men his age will be called to fight; his argument is that he might as well go now rather than waiting.

WILFRED:

(*right center*) It hasn't stopped altogether—don't you hear?

[MRS. VARNEY. (*center*) Yes, but compared to what it was yesterday—you know it shook the house. Howard suffered dreadfully! (*Wilfred suddenly faces her*)]

WILFRED: So did I, Mother! (*Slight pause*) (*Low boom of cannon*)

[MRS. VARNEY. You!]

WILFRED. When I hear those guns and know the fighting's on, it makes me——

[MRS. VARNEY. (*Goes toward table left center. Interrupting quickly*) Yes yes—we all suffered—we all suffered dear! (*Sits right of table left center*)]

WILFRED. Mother—you may not like it but you must listen—(*Going toward her*)—you must let me tell you how——

[MRS. VARNEY. Wilfred! (*He stops speaking.—She takes his hand in hers tenderly.—A brief pause*) I know.]

WILFRED. (*Low pleading voice*) But it's true Mother! I can't stay back here any longer! It's worse than being shot to pieces! I can't do it! (*Mrs. Varney looks steadily into Wilfred's face but says nothing. Soon she turns away a little as if she felt tears coming into her eyes*) Why don't you speak?

[MRS. VARNEY. (*Turning to him. A faint attempt to smile*) I don't know what to say.]

WILFRED. Say you won't mind if I go down there and help 'em!

[MRS. VARNEY. It wouldn't be true!]

WILFRED. I can't stay here!

[MRS. VARNEY. You're so young!]

WILFRED. No younger then Tom Kittridge—no younger than Ell Stuart—nor cousin Stephen—nor hundreds of the fellows fighting down there!—See Mother—they've called for all over eighteen—that was weeks ago! The seventeen call may be out any minute—the next one after that takes me! Do I want to stay back here till they *order* me out! I should think not! (*Walks about to center. Stops and speaks to Mrs. Varney*) If I was hit with a shell an' *had* to stay it would be different! But I can't stand this—I can't do it Mother!

Questions

1. Why do you think Wilfred would want so much to join the Confederate Army?

2. How do you think Wilfred views the world—realistically or idealistically? Explain.

3. Do you think the mother should oppose Wilfred's wanting to join the Confederate Army?

4. What emotions do you think Wilfred is feeling in this scene?

5. How would you feel if you had to join a fighting army at age sixteen?

Monologues
for Females

Millennium

Ted Miller/ *U.S.A.*

This monologue is one of many from *My End Is My Beginning,* a performance piece—a series of monologues that deals with reincarnation. Characters in the monologues come from a variety of time periods and cultures. The unifying theme is that they all are past lives of Edward, who gives the final monologue. The central idea is that Edward's past lives, both male and female, help him understand and cope with the present.

In this scene, Vida accompanies her husband because she had no choice in the matter. During the historical period in which this scene takes place, a woman was expected to obey her husband.

If the piece is too long, you can cut a minute off by ending with the line "from which he and Jerome had tumbled." You also can cut the beginning and begin with "Jerome decided that Stuart and I would accompany him . . ."

VIDA:

My marriage to Jerome Maugham admittedly was a failure. Never could I reach him. Perhaps he would say the same of me. I do not know. We never discussed it. There was nothing, in fact, we did discuss.

I did not love Jerome. I thought once I did, when we married and set up our home outside of London in the year of our Lord 994, but I was wrong. Under the same roof we went our separate ways. I looked after Stuart, our son, as Jerome became more and more wrapped up in his study of religion.

Sometimes, late at night, I looked in on him. He would be reading, shuffling through a pile of manuscripts, his thin shoulders hunched, his eyes intense with religious fervor. He looked for all the world like a miser hoarding money. More and more he lived in the past.

Maybe, had I tried harder, I could have made a success of my marriage to Jerome. In the first year I did try, before the birth of our son. A bride of fifteen, I set my ideals too high. I looked upon Jerome, at twenty-two, as a man of sophistication. But he was not. He cared about little but his studies, working the fields by day and burning the lamps by night. Often days would pass with hardly a word between us.

Maybe, too, had Stuart not been so afflicted, requiring constant care, I could have devoted more attention to Jerome. But then, I suppose, it became too late. I was filled with good reasons which by light of day became excuses.

Jerome decided that Stuart and I would accompany him on the end of the world pilgrimage to Jerusalem. Despite official denouncement by the church itself, there was a growing belief throughout England that the millennium mentioned in Revelations XX of the Holy Scriptures would occur on the New Year's Eve. There would be great happiness as the risen Christ took His rightful place and ruled the earth. Men, women and children clustered throughout England to join thousands of other pilgrims, including serfs and knights, bound for the long journey to Mount Zion.

Stuart's condition being as it was, I fought against going. Jerome insisted that there was a strong possibility of Stuart's being healed. No, not a possibility, a conviction.

Almost since infancy, Stuart had been afflicted. Despite many attempts to disguise the fact from Jerome, from Stuart, and most of all from myself, Stuart's condition seemed to worsen with each passing day.

"He'll outgrow it," I'd tell Jerome. "A great many children outgrow it." Jerome would look at me quizzically. He said nothing.

Stuart would suddenly lose consciousness. Then there would be a series of spasms throughout his body. Afterwards, he would fall into a heavy sleep that lasted for hours. It would be so deep he'd appear to be dead.

Were I finally able to rouse him, he would be extremely irritable, striking out blindly. Sometimes, too, were I not careful, Stuart would awaken from his sleep, or rather *seem* to do so, then wander off. Often he became lost. If anyone questioned him, he wouldn't or couldn't answer. If touched accidentally by others while in this state, Stuart sometimes flew into a rage, beating on them unmercifully.

Fortunately, at the age of five, he was not a large child. However, I could not see us going on such a trip as Jerome proposed. I knew it would be an almost impossible task to manage Stuart. Jerome attempted to reassure me.

"Suppose Stuart has a spell? How will we keep up with the group?" I asked.

"I'll carry him," Jerome responded. "You'll see."

"Why do you *want* to go?" I asked.

"I have to," Jerome answered.

"Sometimes when Stuart has a spell," I objected, "he soils himself."

"We'll carry extra clothing for him."

Seeing my look, he interpreted it correctly. "Oh, I'll carry those too."

Against my better judgment, hoping for a reprieve in some unknown fashion, I reluctantly prepared for the journey, perhaps as a recompense for not loving Jerome. We each took one change of clothing, and, of course, our capes. It would be too difficult to carry more.

Many not going on the pilgrimage reaped a plentiful harvest as they purchased bargains in furniture, clothing, livestock and homes. The pilgrims sold them cheaply or gave them away in order to guarantee themselves a place in paradise. They were aware of how a rich man is likened to a camel going through a needle's eye.

" 'Behold the lilies of the field,' " said some of the holy men as they asked for the money the pilgrims had received " 'They toil not, neither do they spin.' You will need none of this. Trust in the Lord. He will take care of you."

Only much later did I discover that many such holy men were themselves remaining behind.

Some pilgrims decided to forgive debts. Merchants, confessing to having cheated customers, gave their money to the holy men as a form of bribery to secure forgiveness. Cautious pilgrims, thinking they could return to their homes if the last judgment did not occur, disposed of nothing. They were in the minority.

"Oh, ye of little faith," taunted the holy men.

Jerome insisted on selling or giving away everything. I, however, appealed to my mother to buy our little cottage for a pittance.

"I'll keep it for you, Vida," she said. "If you return, it will be waiting, just as you left it."

Mother refused to accompany us. She prepared a tasty meal of beef and kidney pie, vegetables and rich desserts, kissed us and gave us her blessing.

But the effects of the food did not last long, and soon our stomachs were empty. We learned that singing disguised the hunger and helped us cover ground quickly.

"There are angels in the sky. In the clouds—with shining trumps. See the angels?" My neighbor shouted.

I saw no angels. Only clouds.

"We shall march, even as the children of Israel marched," Jerome announced. "There shall be a pillar of fire before us by night, a pillar of smoke by day."

"You don't really believe that, do you?" I asked him. He did not reply.

"God summons us to His Day of Judgment," another pilgrim declared. "For is it not written that God shall reign for one thousand years over a new earth?"

"The spirits of the Holy Apostles shall lead us through deep valleys and over high mountains," a third pilgrim said.

"Oh, yes," another joined in. "We shall live as they lived so long ago."

"Before we reach our goal," one of the holy men continued, "some of you may die. But have no fear. For those who die are blessed. Their soul shall prepare a placed for those of us who follow."

The holy man was right. By the thousands the marchers died from starvation, exposure and illness. First were the elderly and those with afflictions.

The journey seemed endless. To pass the time, I taught psalms and canticles to Stuart. Jerome was true to his word. He carried our son, often lingering behind when Stuart had fits. At first the weather was balmy and warm. Quickly, autumn was upon us. At night we shivered, stretched out on the ground, huddled close for warmth.

Some superstitious folk looked upon Stuart as being possessed by Satan. Others disagreed; they claimed him blessed by God, seeing visions denied the rest of us.

Sometimes our band divided; one segment went one way, the rest another. Sometimes we met groups coming from other villages and towns. At times it was necessary for carts traveling to market to take to the fields as we straggled past. After a time, the villages all looked alike, and all we could contemplate was the next step we would take and the next.

Over rivers and through mountainous country we journeyed. A few were lost in the raging waters that nearly swept us off our feet. I grasped Jerome more tightly around the waist and followed his sure-footed progress. Malnourished and weak, we began to rest more often for longer and longer periods.

Across high ranges covered with forests and vineyards, their summits castle-crowned, we struggled. Under other circumstances I might have paused to view the colored leaves on the trees or the lightly falling snow. Instead, these hurried us on our way, foretelling of the hardships of approaching winter. In each meadow through which we passed the crows cawed noisily, their voices seeming to call "Fool, fool, you. Fool."

Bit by bit, I became accustomed to what I saw. I stared at my surroundings less and less while those we passed stared at us. My once lovely clothing was soiled and shoddy, as was that of all the pilgrims. I resented the shabbiness.

Sometimes farmers pressed upon us the produce from their fields, apologetic for not joining the pilgrimage. Others scoffed at us, calling us dreamers and fanatics.

I wished I could leave the pilgrimage and remain on some pleasant spot, but from childhood it had been impressed on me that a wife's place is beside her husband. In my bitterness, blaming Jerome, yet not saying a thing to him, I suspect I showed my frustrations in other ways. Poor man. He took all I did without complaint.

Every time there was a heavy storm, the sighting of a meteor, a minor trembling of the earth, a high wind, there was panic among the pilgrims. Frightened, weeping, everywhere people asked one another: "Is it happening?"

"God is angry," said some, hearing thunder. Falling to their knees, rain pelting down upon them, they sought God's grace with outstretched arms.

"Our Father, Who art in heaven," they prayed, "Forgive us if we have offended Thee."

Finally, Jerome told me we had arrived in Mount Zion. As we climbed to the top, I saw that many friends and neighbors who'd started the journey were absent. Some, I know, had dropped out to return home. Most of the missing had died en route. My eyes filled with tears.

A hush descended on the throng as we knelt and prayed. It reminded me in an insane way of how an audience conducts itself while waiting for a group of strolling players to begin their performance after all have assembled.

But the show did not begin.

"They didn't figure time in Biblical days like they do today," said the holy men.

So we waited for days on end for Jesus to come. The old year ended; the new began.

Disheartened, disenchanted, many families began the long trip back. Some talked of settling in communities they had seen along the way, rather than facing the comments they expected at home. Others felt that since God had not judged them, they might as well have a good time until He did.

Jerome was depressed. He realized that he had insisted on bringing Stuart and me from the relative comforts of home through unspeakable hardship for no useful purpose whatever.

"Mother will let us have our cottage back." I finally told him, hoping to cheer him up a bit as we walked along. He refused to be cheered.

On our way home, Stuart had one spell after another. Jerome improvised a sling to carry him. Still we lagged behind. As we traveled through a mountainous region, Stuart had a violent seizure in Jerome's arms. He flailed about wildly, kicking and hitting at his father. I tried to calm him, and his violence only increased.

Jerome made a misstep on the narrow path. Stuart in his arms, he tumbled down the precipice. I saw them sprawled at the bottom, far below. Stuart had landed on the bundle of supplies and appeared unhurt. Jerome's body lay crumpled and still.

"Jerome," I called, "Jerome, answer me. Are you all right?"

I knew the words were inane. I could tell he was not all right. He responded with a groan that reached me at the top of the cliff.

"I'll get somebody," I called. Then yelled wildly to the pilgrims in the distance. No one bothered to answer.

I slid and stumbled down the mountainside.

"I tried," Jerome gasped, unable to rise. "Oh, God, Vida, you'll never know how I tried."

I pillowed his head in my arms. He told me how his father, his grandfather, his uncle and his brother all had spells similar to Stuart's. He told me I shouldn't reproach myself. Instead, he was the one to blame in never having told me.

"There were many things I should have told you," he said. "Such as how much I love you. You never thought I did, I know, but I loved you more than anybody in the world."

"Shhhh," I said. "I know now. Save your strength."

"How is Stuart? Is he hurt?"

"I'll see," I said and looked at my son. "He's sleeping peacefully. You cushioned his fall."

"I see it now," he whispered.

"What is it you see?" I asked.

"The last judgment. The last judgment." He gasped, shuddered slightly and died in my arms.

As vultures circled, I gathered stones to cover his body. Perhaps I was too numb with fatigue to feel much of anything.

I bent down and picked up Stuart. "Sleep, baby, sleep," I whispered.

He looked serene in my arms. I discarded some of our belongings and managed to carry Stuart to the path from which he and Jerome had tumbled.

The procession was nowhere to be seen. Perhaps when they rested, I'd be able to overtake them.

Hurrying to catch up, I was waylaid by a gang of ruffians. One of them took Stuart from my arms and laid him down. They said they were going to rob me. I told them I had nothing, but they refused to believe me. When they found it was true, they hit me, knocking me down.

I glanced at Stuart who lay nearby, his face pressed into the ground. Crawling toward him, I tried to gather him up. One of the men laughed and told me Stuart was dead. I refused to believe him. Yet when I examined him more closely, I saw that it was true.

I tried to bury him as best I could, as I had Jerome. Then I made my way back to my native village. The little cottage where we had lived was in ruin. Mother was nowhere to be found. There were famine and plague. Thousands of people were dying throughout the land. I knew I would soon be one of them.

Questions

1. Why do you think Vida finally agreed to accompany Jerome on the pilgrimage?

2. Such a pilgrimage as this actually did occur during this time period. Why do you think so many people felt it better to go on the pilgrimage than stay at home for the expected end of the world?

3. Is Vida a believable person? Why? Do you sympathize with her?

4. What really was wrong with Stuart? Why do you think Vida tried to hide his illness?

5. Why does Vida say she knows she's going to be one of the people who will soon die?

Playing time: Six minutes to six minutes and 30 seconds
Character's age: 18

Hattie B. Moore

from the play *Eden Creek*
Dwight Watson/ *U.S.A.*

"*H*attie B. Moore," although set in the 1930s, deals with a situation that still is with us—a child being born to an unwed mother. In this instance, Hattie has decided to give the child away.

Eden Creek is similar to *Millennium* in that it is a series of monologues. Before this monologue begins, Hattie slips a jacket over her blouse and straightens her coat. "She moves her hat to a table beside the bed, opens her suitcase, and packs as she talks to a lady from the county health agency." The woman is seated in a chair in the corner as Hattie, "with light but purposeful movements, prepares to leave." In this piece the woman from the agency is an imaginary character.

HATTIE:

(*Quickly*) I hope you don't mind if I pack while we talk. I want to keep busy, you understand. The doctor told me you were from the county welfare agency. (*Packing the suitcase*) She said I would have to sign some papers . . . answer some questions before the clinic would release me. Mom said I was never shy with words. She said I talked so much I should be on the radio. (*Slightly embarrassed*) It's true. I do love to talk. I won the Eden Creek speech contest in the seventh grade for a dramatic recitation I called "The Day I Danced With Harlequin." I ended the speech with the poem "Harlequin" by Arthur Guiterman. (*She smiles*) I still remember some of the lines.

(*Hattie steps forward, prepares herself and recites the poem using gentle and previously rehearsed gestures.*)

"This body, now a gallant robe, is frayed:
I must withdraw a while to put it by
And don a new, wherein I'll masquerade
So well that none will guess that I am I."

(*She finishes the recitation and gives a somewhat self-conscious shrug in the direction of the lady before resuming her packing.*)

I left school at the end of that year because my dad left home. We haven't seen him since. Mom needed me to work around the house and to take care of my baby brothers so that she could get a job. For three years I took care of the house. (*Opens her purse*) I hated it and decided then that I would never have children. (*Searching for a pen, she looks to the lady*) Are these the papers? Pencil or pen? Does it matter? Pen? Yes, I have my own. (*She sits on the bed*) I didn't complain much to Mom. We were like sisters. Sometimes, late at night, we would talk about private things like the love between men and women. (*Confidentially*) I remember once she said, "Hattie, some day you might decide to marry. And if you don't want butter, then you'd better learn to pull the dasher out in time." (*Slight pause*) She knew that I wasn't interested in having children. (*Finds the pen*) Here it is. I dreamed of seeing the world. (*She cracks a smile*) I'd been writing to a girlfriend, Doris, who used to live in Eden Creek but now she lives and works in Chicago. Doris invited me to stay with her for a few days so that I could see the Chicago World's Fair. I was dying to go and my Mom knew it. (*She rises*) One day Mom came home from work and handed me an envelope with a bus ticket . . . to Chicago!

(*Hattie places the pen by the papers and moves to her suitcase.*)

The next day I packed my best clothes and a lunch and was on my way. When that bus pulled into the Chicago Bus Terminal, I thought I would explode from happiness! Doris, my girlfriend, met me at the bus station and then took me to her apartment. We spent that evening together. She wanted to talk about Eden Creek, but I was so excited about Chicago that I could think of nothing else. The next morning Doris had to go to work. (*With growing anticipation*) I made my way to the exhibition ground. (*Pause. Seeing the sign*) It was called A CENTURY OF PROGRESS, and I was there the day the gates opened. June 1, 1933. I wanted to be there early to hear the opening address on what was said to be the "World's Largest Loud Speaker," specially built for the fair. I remember this man talked about the greatness of Chicago. He talked about how Chicago had pulled itself out of the swamp, and how Chicago had survived and recovered from the great fire. (*Hearing his voice*) He kept using the words "courage" and "enterprise" over and over to describe the character of Chicago. "Courage and enterprise." "In the middle of the Depression it takes a city of courage and enterprise to build a World's Fair."

After he had finished this speech, I just wanted to go up to the "world's largest loud speaker" and announce to everyone, "I'm happy to be here!" (*She moves to the table*) I spent the rest of that morning in the Field Museum of Natural History and that afternoon I toured the Shedd Aquarium. (*Slight pause*) I was standing by that huge glass tank staring at all those strange fish when a young man, a man I'd seen earlier that day at the Field Museum, struck up a conversation. He was very handsome and very eager to talk. There was just so much to see and so much to talk about, I was delighted when he asked if he could be my escort. He said he had recently been discharged from the military service and that he was taking a few days to see the fair before going to work. We walked and talked for hours. I remember he asked me what I wanted from life. (*Moving to the bed*) I told him I just wanted to travel all over the world and to introduce myself to every human being. (*Extending her hand*) "Hello, I'm Hattie B. Moore from Eden Creek!" He must've thought that was kinda funny because he began calling me not just Hattie, but Hattie B. Moore. He said that Hattie B. Moore was the name of a beautiful riverboat that carried passengers up and down the lengths of the great Mississippi. And that while I was in Chicago I was to be his Hattie B. Moore. (*Slight pause*) You know, it's funny, because my Mom's maiden name is Moore, and somehow it seemed right that I adopted her maiden name instead of the name of the father who left me.

(*She moves slowly around room attempting to recapture the feeling.*)

For three days we walked all over the city of Chicago. For two of those three days we held hands and walked all over the city of Chicago. Finally, on my last day at the fair, I told my escort that Hattie B. Moore wanted to stroll up and down the lengths of Michigan Avenue. Then as evening approached, and all of the city lights were on, I decided to ride what was said to be the greatest amusement attraction ever! (*Looking upward*) The Sky Ride. (*Closing her eyes*) My escort said that he would be glad to travel to the top of the Sky Ride Tower with me if I would . . . . (*She stops—catching herself*) (*Pause*) That night . . . we rode six hundred feet to the top of the Sky Ride Tower. The view took my breath away. My escort kissed me and that took my breath away. Four hundred feet below us we could see the Sky Ride Rocket cars, made of glass and spewing red and white smoke. They carried passengers to a tower some two thousand feet away.

(*Pause*) It's hard to describe the feeling. (*Pause*) I spent the night with that man. (*Slight pause*) It's hard to describe the feeling. But then I had never been to a big city. (*With growing excitement*) I had never seen so many tall buildings. Never been to a museum, or even knew what an aquarium or planetarium was. And I never dreamed there could be such a thing as a tower six hundred feet in the air!

(*Pause. She sits and slowly picks up the pen.*)

When I came home to Eden Creek, nothing had changed. My Mom still needed me. There was no one else to look after the house or her children. And I knew then our tiny house could not hold another child.

(*Hattie signs the forms, leaves them on the table, and slowly moves to the other side of the room. She shows a quiet resolve, emotional but strong.*)

You know, in a few years I'm going to travel all over the world. I am. I'm going to break away from Eden Creek or break my neck trying. That is why this baby cannot stay with me. There is no room in my life or in my mother's house for one more child. (*Pause. Closes her suitcase*) I held her this morning. She is beautiful. But ma'am, the way I see it, you can hold them for five minutes or fifteen years, but sooner or later you are forced to let them go. (*Pause*) And whether you know it or not, I do feel for her in my heart. But when I left

Chicago, (*Picking up the suitcase and hat*) I was touched by A CEN-
TURY OF PROGRESS. I'm no longer Hattie from Eden Creek. (*As
if donning a new name*) I am Hattie B. Moore.

Questions

1. Why do you think Hattie wanted so much to get away from home?
   Why was she so impressed with the World's Fair?

2. Why do you suppose Hattie's mother let her go to Chicago when
   she was needed so badly at home?

3. How do you think Hattie feels about giving away her baby? What
   makes you think so?

4. What do you think the rest of Hattie's life will be like? Why?

5. How would you describe in a sentence or two the type of person
   Hattie is?

The Misfit

Karen Carriere / *U.S.A.*

The monologue is excerpted from a longer piece about peer pressure. Lalani is expected to help acquaint the daughter of her mother's friend with the school she attends and with her friends. Yet Annie May doesn't meet any of the standards that Lalani thinks are important.

The monologue shows a clash between two different ways of thinking, between two girls who have grown up in different parts of the country.

In a scene that preceded this one, Lalani was dreading the appearance of Annie May. This shows what happens when the two characters first meet.

LALANI:

I was just catching the latch on my locket when they walked in, and it's a good thing, too, that my head was down cause what I saw when I looked up was enough to bring nightmares to Eddie Jefferson, and he still said "y'all" and ate grits with gravy.

She had on a thin cotton dress, gray, with no lace and no collar, not even no buttons that I could see, but with big flowers on it with yellow stems. She did have on two thick red knee socks, although they didn't really look like a pair with one loose and dropped down to her ankles showing spotty brown calves below two of the chalki-est, volcano-white knees I had ever seen. She had on glasses, not the kind Evita wears with the tortoise-shell frames, but white ones that was pinched and curved up at the ends, like the Catlady's on "Batman," and with masking tape wrapped on one side. Her eyes was like big, chestnut circles, that is, what I could see of them when she wasn't looking down at the carpet or her knees or her scruffed up patent leather shoes. Her hair should have been cute, since it was thick and autumn-colored, what Mama calls "cellophane," but it was bunched up in about six sections with no parts or barrettes or noth-ing, just those green rubber bands they use to tie up newspapers. She had on this long, droopy sweater that would have been too big on Mama if she had tried it on, with stray threads sticking out all over the place. And she kept biting on her bottom lip or rubbing her eye making her glasses tip down her nose or playing with this gold chain on her wrist, twisting it around her fingers till her skin was white and had rings all around it.

I dropped my necklace on the floor, and Mama picked it up and fastened it for me.

"This is Annie May, sweetheart," she said resting her arm around Annie May's shoulder. Honey was rolling around in Mama's mouth like it always did when she was talking about somebody from "down home." "Her mother says she's a little quiet sometimes but she is looking forward to going to school in San Francisco. Tell her hello."

I didn't even like looking at her. She was messed up from head to toe, and I was gonna have to be with her all day. My mama is real thin and not much taller than me. People say all the time that we almost look like sisters. Well, Mama might be alright sometimes, and she could tell a good joke when she wanted to, but deep down inside Mama was still mama, a wicked witch with a vacuum cleaner, and I had to pay the price.

Usually I take the bus to school. It comes by Edison Elementary around the corner at 8:15 every morning. But today I figured I'd just walk. We could go around back of the fire station and walk up Palm Street by the hospital. Not too many people went that way, not unless they had a bike or a skateboard to ride, cause it took longer, and there was a lot of traffic on the street. Daddy took that way to the freeway every morning, but he had already left so he wouldn't see me. He would probably wonder why I didn't just take her to the bus stop where everybody was at before school.

Anyway, it was gonna be a long day, and I wanted to get rolling so I grabbed my books and headed out the door before Mama could say anything else. Annie May waved to Mama as she shuffled down the stairs after me. I was walking kinda fast 'cause I forgot how long it takes to get there when you go that way, and Annie May was just scuttling along, behind me and to the side, kinda close to the street. When I slowed down so she could catch up, she slowed down, too, dropping even farther behind me. When I walked faster, you could hear those black tap shoes clippity-clop to keep up, but she never pulled ahead of me, just stayed some distance behind. The sash on her dress kept coming undone and dragging on the streets. Every few minutes she'd pick it up and tie it in a big bow on the side of her dress only to see it drop back down two seconds later, sweeping the street again. She looked like some stray puppy somebody had found and dropped off on the wrong side of town.

We had got past the hardware store, and Annie May hadn't said a word. If it wasn't for those noisy shoes, I'd've thought I'd lost her. It became obvious that she wasn't gonna be the first to speak so I figured I might as well get it over with.

"New dress?" Mama would've popped me for that smart-mouthed comment.

"Not really. My mother made it for me," she said, kinda shocked like the teacher had called on her when she wasn't ready. "The sleeves are from some pillow shams I had in my room in Natchitoches."

She saw me grinning while I waited for the light to change. She looked at my sweater, then back at her dress. "I think it's a very nice dress," she said, finally and kinda defiant like, and went back to jingling her bracelet.

"Why did you leave Louisiana anyway?" It was the main thing I wanted to know, and she wasn't gonna volunteer no information.

Plus, Mama had always acted like Natchitoches was such a cozy place to live that only the war was able to pull her away.

"My mother wanted to stay in Natchitoches," she said in a low, dewy voice, talking to her shoes. "But our money from the army was running out, and mother couldn't get a job there until next September." She pressed her lips together like she was being quizzed by the host of some TV game show and was getting ready for the next round of questions.

"Why you come to California? To be around us. I know your mama and my mama used to be friends."

"Well, mother was able to find a job here. She hasn't worked since before I was born."

Even though she had a country accent there was something proper about the way she talked, like a grown-up or like the way people talk when the minister is listening.

"California isn't as warm as I thought it would be," she volunteered suddenly. "In Natchitoches, on the way to school the heat would come up through your shoes like fire. In California it's cold in the morning, and the air is so fuzzy I don't know how people can see." She pushed her glasses back up on her nose.

"That's the fog off the bay. It'll burn off by second period or so."

"What do you and your friends like to do?" she asked, dropping farther behind me.

I was afraid this would happen, and I had a funny feeling that the answer to that question was all she really cared about. Not only was I gonna have to entertain her at school, but I was gonna have to take care of her after school activities, too.

"I practice, mostly, drill team, and glee club on Wednesdays. You gotta be in the club to stay in the rec room during practice, though." Maybe that would do it. Get her mind from that mine field quick.

"I used to play the flute in our marching band back home," she says. It was hard to imagine. She seemed so awkward and lightfooted now. "But I like the piano better."

"You can play the piano?" Two instruments? Well, like Mama says, looks don't tell you everything.

"Oh, yes," she says, and she looked me in the face for the first time. "My daddy taught me how when I was in the second grade." She even skipped up a few paces so there wasn't so much space between us while we walked. "When he was home we used to play almost every night. We took turns or even played at the same time. Some songs sound good that way."

"Well, what happened to him? Where is your daddy?" She dropped back a few steps and sank her hands into her pockets.

"He got lost in Viet Nam."

"Got lost? What do you mean he got lost?"

"I don't know. They sent him to do something, an' they couldn't find him later."

"Didn't somebody look for him?"

"Uh, huh," she says, nodding her head. "But where he was is just like a jungle my mother says."

I didn't see how anybody could get that lost. I been lost plenty of times, but somebody always found me. Once when I was in Disneyland I got lost from my Girl Scout troop. It took Mrs. Davidson almost two hours to find me, and when she did I was busy drinking pop and eating juju bees, free from the lady at the snack booth. But I guess if you get lost in a jungle you gotta be the one to do the finding. People probably ain't in too much of a hurry to find you.

"I can teach you to play sometime," she says, curling up into a little ball again and her voice dropping to a whisper, "If you want."

Questions

1. How would you feel if you were expected to show a new person like Annie May around school?

2. Why do you think Lalani is so critical of Annie May's speech and dress? Is she justified in feeling this way?

3. Why is it so important for Lalani to fit in, to be like her friends?

4. What are the things that Lalani admired about Annie May? Why do you suppose she did?

5. Do you like Lalani? Why? What kind of person is she?

Playing time: Four minutes and 30 seconds to
five minutes
Character's age: Probably about 20

Giantess

Mimi Albert/ *U.S.A.*

Giantess, like *The Misfit,* is a performance piece about fitting in or being accepted. Miranda, the main character, is sound mentally, but because of her grotesque appearance, nobody will accept her as having normal intelligence. She is institutionalized after her mother dies.

Miranda is very big and her head is misshapen. In the piece, she says: "I'm almost seven feet tall and broad to match. My skull keeps growing and my nose and forehead are so thick you can hardly see my eyes, which gives me a dull and stupid look."

MIRANDA:

My mother and I lived in an old, low-rent apartment on one of these streets together until she died. First I remember being a child, being dragged from doctor to doctor. Later I was a grown woman and she got sick. When I'd put my coat on to go out for a walk, she'd always yell, "Where you going now?" (She didn't like me to go out where the neighbors could see me. I had to sneak.) "Why walk the street out in broad daylight? What do you think you're going to find?"

Well, she was right. I was looking for something, and I thought I'd find it out there, out in the city. I dreamed about it too, though I was never sure what I wanted. I listened to music on the radio and music did something inside me. It was listening to the music that let me walk the streets. Why didn't anybody ever see the music inside me when I walked?

At home, when I could get away from my mother's anger and prying, I read all the time. Not just romances, trash, the kind of books they expect a young girl to read, but also good novels, biographies. Poetry. Books on art. Later on, when illness made her less angry, I would read to her sometimes too. We were lonely and poor but there was still a roof over our heads. That made a difference. And we had each other. Odd, how it changed between us just when it was about to end.

"The artist is the true child of his people," said the old poet as I listened, rapt and startled. How his words sank into me. Could he have known? Lifting his eyes, he might have seen me, my face already huge and monstrous, but feeling a mantle of beauty falling over me as he spoke.

"But he is his people's stepchild, too, and when he looks at the ones with whom he shares his life, he brings a stepchild's pain and understanding to them, a stepchild's love. So if you want to be an artist, a poet, then you must be both child and stepchild of your race."

One of my teachers had taken me to hear him. There were a few teachers who really cared about me, and this one had given up her Sunday to take me to hear this talk. She changed my life. By the time I got home, I was so worked up that my cheeks burned red and my mother thought I had a fever.

"Never mind that," I told her when she came at me with the thermometer. "I'm just happy, that's all."

He was an old poet and he hardly looked at me but it didn't matter. I understood him. What else was I but the child and stepchild of my people? I bought a notebook and began to write.

"The first thing she ever remembered hearing her mother calling her was 'Monster,'" I wrote. "'Monster, Monster,' said her mother. 'Why did I give birth to you?'

"She was a normal kid in most ways and at first she thought that she was pretty, even beautiful when she played and danced with other children. There were other children before she got too big. She had a costume made from a white silk dress some older cousin or friend had left for her. At seven, she stumbled around the house in her mother's shoes. She thought she was like others and, except for an occasional pain and too many visits to too many doctors, she felt no different.

"One day she began to realize that no other children wanted to play with her. Sometimes they even ran away from her, screaming, and once some boys threw rocks at her from a tree. She was very strong and big and she twisted the arm of one of the boys behind his back, but it didn't help the sadness that she felt when she was hit or when her mother called her 'Monster' or when, sometimes, she fell and couldn't get up by herself because her limbs were so thick and strange. And sometimes now she had an awful pain in her head and knees.

"Her mother took her to even more doctors and she hated them all, and she hated it whenever her mother asked in an angry voice, 'Can't you do anything to stop her from growing?' But even though they tried lots of things like radiation and surgery, things that hurt, nothing ever did.

And then one day when she was alone, she looked into a mirror and then, for the first time, she saw, she really saw. . . ."

I wrote so quickly and with such excitement that I had to buy another notebook the next day which was also quickly filled. (I really like the line about the limbs being thick and strange.) But the trouble was I had nothing much to write about. Nothing had ever happened to me except to be born myself. I had read about adventure and romance, but I had never experienced either. I dreamed of how good it might be to kiss someone, to feel something against my lips besides my own teeth. But when I tried to write down my fantasies, they came out unreal. I could write only about being a sad, young woman who was ugly, whose mother called her "Monster," and from whom other children ran away, screaming, "Here she comes! The Giantess!"

Questions

1. Why do you think no one would look beyond the physical ugliness to the person inside Miranda's body?

2. What do you think Miranda is feeling in this monologue? Why?

3. Would you befriend Miranda? Why?

4. What is the prevailing mood of this monologue? Explain.

5. What do you suppose the rest of Miranda's life will be like?

Playing time: One minute 55 seconds to two minutes and 15 seconds
Character's age: About 15

My Sister in This House

Wendy Kesselman/ *U.S.A.*

The play is based on a true story about two sisters, Christine and Lea Papin, who murdered the mistress and daughter of the house they worked in as maids.

This monologue is the opening scene of the play, set in Le Mans, France, during the early 1930s.

LEA:

Dear Christine. When Maman left me here on Friday, I thought I would die. They didn't want to take me at first, but Maman told Madame Crespelle I was fifteen. Christine, I wish you could see what they eat. You can't imagine the desserts. The cook told me Madame's favorite dish is duck with cherries and Monsieur's, chicken with champagne. I'm hungry all the time. But it isn't as bad as I expected. I even have my own room. Do you think you could ask Madame Roussel to change your day off to Wednesday, like mine? (*She pauses.*) Today Madame Crespelle smiled at me. She was pleased with how the silver looked. I had been polishing it all morning. It was worth every minute for Madame's smile. When she smiles she looks just like Sister Veronica. (*A bell rings. Lea moves closer to Christine.*) Three days ago Maman came and took me away. She said I could earn money somewhere else. I was just getting used to the Crespelles, but I'm getting four more francs a month and Maman's promised to let me keep one of them. The Cottins have one daughter, Mademoiselle Sophie. Her birthday is next week. She's only two months older than me. She's so pretty. Her skin is like milk. And Christine, you should hear her play the piano. (*She pauses.*) Madame Cottin counts everything. Even the chocolates in the glass bowl. But I remember everything you taught me. And I think Madame will be pleased with me. (*She pauses.*) Every morning Madame Cottin examines my fingernails before I make the beds. Her things are so delicate. So many ruffles. So many buttons. You wouldn't believe how many buttons. It takes me two hours to iron one dress. And even then Madame isn't satisfied. (*She pauses.*) In this house I'm always afraid I'll do something wrong. Not like you, Christine. You never make mistakes. (*She pauses. Longingly.*) Oh Christine, if only Maman would place us together. (*A bell rings, almost interrupting Lea's last sentence. Lea goes down to her hands and knees and begins polishing the floor. Christine looks out.*)

Questions

1. How do you think Lea feels about the things she observes in the two places she worked? Which place does she like better? How can you tell?

2. Do you think Lea likes her job? Why?

3. What sort of person do you think Lea is? Why?

4. Why do you think Lea wishes she and Christine could work together?

5. What word would you use to describe the mood of this scene?

Playing time: Ten minutes and 30 seconds to eleven minutes and 30 seconds
Character's age: 17

The Monologue

Marla Bentz/*U.S.A.*

Another performance piece, "The Monologue" is complete in itself and is a tale of someone going to a professional audition for a major role for the first time. The following is just a slice of the whole performance.

The following monologue is an exaggeration or an enlargement upon what really might happen when someone is auditioning to be a member of a company that does performance pieces.

(So far as ethnic background, race or religion, Sarah is whatever she wants to be.)

SARAH:

Hi, I'm Sarah Walker. Why did I say that? You know that already. I think you know that already. This is the first time I've ever auditioned. Professionally, I mean. School plays, church, things like that. I auditioned a lot of times for things like that, but never—I'm sorry, I already said that.

You want me to tell you about myself. God, I don't know what to tell you. I'm seventeen. I graduated from the school of performing arts last month—Oh, yeah, I guess I did audition professionally. I mean I was in the chorus of a musical. But that hardly counts, does it? I mean nearly everyone in my class was in the chorus of that musical. And it closed after one night. It closed after half a night. 'Cause everyone walked out. Right in the middle of a number. Like a trail of ants. They trickled right out. And there we were, singing and dancing and . . .

I was born . . . I mean, this might be interesting. I was born in Liechtenstein. There aren't many foreigners born in Liechtenstein. Not many *people* born in Liechtenstein. Not many people *living* in Liechtenstein.

See, my parents were on this trip, and I was born early, and I was born in . . . I already said that.

I came home when I was a week old. To British Columbia. Maybe I should explain that. My dad was working in British Columbia. I mean I'm not Canadian. Not that there's anything wrong with being Canadian. I'm not a Liechtenstinian eith—is that the word? Liechtenstinian?

Sorry, I'm babbling.

Mom said she thought I started performing the day I was born. She was just kidding, of course, but I can't remember when I didn't want to be an actress. Oh, God, I thought. It would be so wonderful.

So anyhow I was always singing and dancing and reciting nursery rhymes. My mom says I knew—the whole "Night before Christmas" when I was a year and a half. A year and a half old, can you imagine? I'd say it at the drop of a pin. That's not right. Drop of a hat. That's right; that's what it is, isn't it?

So anyhow I started singing and reciting poems and things in school and church and family reunions—I was never nervous. You might think I'm nervous. But I was never nervous. High-strung like a thoroughbred. That's what Dad said. He didn't know anything about horses. Never even saw a race. That's what he told me.

You're letting me babble on here. (*Laughs nervously*) So maybe I could recite something. How about it? What do you say? Can I recite something?

Nah, I better not. You want to hear about my life. Well, there's nothing important. I grew up in—Oh, yeah, I used to play the accordion. Squeeze box is what Grandma called it. (*Broadly pantomimes the words*) Eeeahhhh, eeeahhhh. Bagpipes. That's what I thought the accordion sounded like. Bagpipes. Same principle, air squeezed in and out to make the sound. Bagpipes are always so, I don't know so . . . so mournful. Like the cry of a lonely siren (*caught up in the mood*) luring sailors to deep, vast graves in the sea.

(*Snapping out of it*) But you don't want to hear about bagpipes; you know about bagpipes. The whole world knows about bagpipes. Maybe not the whole world.

(*Takes a deep breath and expels it*) Where was I? Oh, yeah, so I grew up in Jersey. Newark. Can you imagine growing up in Newark? I didn't really grow up in Newark. I moved here when I was thirteen. I mean when I found out about the school of performing arts, and that the kids there got to audition for shows. Professional shows. Wow, you know. Anyhow, I came to stay with my grandma. And I went home weekends, except when I was in a (*exaggerated French accent*) tragédie ou comédie ou a lettle chanson ou danse nombair. (*Serious*) I didn't really want to go home. It was so strange going home. Back into all that—

I'm making a fool of myself up here. Isn't that what I'm doing? Making a fool of myself. Well, so what? You wanted to hear me talk; you wanted to here me sing and act. Did you want to hear me sing?

I don't have any brothers and sisters. Mom says who could put up with another one like me? She was just kidding . . . I think. (*Laughs and points straight ahead*) Of course, she was kidding. (*Serious again*) Except I know she and Dad would have been much happier if—I didn't ask them to be born, did I? I mean—

(*Brightly*) Say, don't I get to read or something? Oh, yeah, the paper you handed me. When I'm done telling you about myself, I'm supposed to read it, act it. But am I done telling you about myself? I mean, I'm done telling you about myself if you want me to be done telling you about myself. But, I can . . . Oh, well.

Yes, now. I see. It's on the paper here. You told me my audition piece was on the paper here. Nothing prepared, you said. A cold reading. Right here on the paper. Okay, here we go. Here it is. (*Reading almost to herself*) "To be or not to be." Oh sure I know that. Everyone knows that. Doesn't everyone know that? (*Reciting in broad Shakespearean tones*) "To be or not to be, that is the question. Whether 'tis nobler in the mind to suffer the slings and arrows of outrageous for—" Hey! Wait a minute here. This is Hamlet. This is a boy. I mean, not a boy, but a man. A young man. Maybe not a boy; he is in college, I think. Isn't he? A college boy. Man. Isn't Hamlet in college somewhere? Sweden, Denmark, something like— Oh, yeah, of course, he's *from* Denmark. He's Danish. Danish? How do you get Danish out of Den—Lochtenstunian! Maybe that's what I'd be if we hadn't come home. To British Columbia. To Newark. To . . . You know, actually I don't know why they brought me home. They never—

Hey, wait! Whoa! Hold everything. The fine print. I see the fine print here. (*Quoting from the imaginary paper from which she'd been reading*) This company was founded for the purpose of expanding gender and ethnic roles.

(*Puzzled*) A Dane is ethnic? So what am I? Aren't I ethnic already? I mean besides the way I look. See the way I look. And you have me playing a Danish white boy? I mean, hey, like they used to say, get with it! Ooh, sorry, I didn't mean anything. Wow, if I say stuff like that—I mean, if I keep on saying stuff like that, I'm going to blow it, aren't I?

So shall we try it again? "To be or not—" Expanding our views and our roles, is that it? You know I kind of admire that. No, really, I mean I do. I really admire that.

So, hey, should I try a little dance step? Why don't I try a little dance step? (*Doing the chorus line bit*) One and a two and a one and a two and a—Remember Lawrence Welk? Oh, God, when I was a little kid, I used to sit in front of the TV set when the "Lawrence Welk Show" came on. I wanted so bad to be one of those sisters, what were their names? You know, the sisters who sang and all that stuff on the

"Lawrence Welk Show"? I envied them so much. And Patty Duke. Remember her as a little girl with her own TV show? And those old movies? Shirley Temple and Margaret O'Brien. I'd give anything if I could have—

Sorry, you don't—I mean. Oh, wow, you've just got to know how important this is to me. It's really important. More important then food and sleeping and . . . well, you know, don't you? Sure, you know, it's like the most important thing in the whole wor—Not really the most important, Mom and Dad, (*Sotto voce*) at least I guess, (*Bright again*) and Grandma—well both Grandmas. And Grandpa.

I never knew my one grandpa. Now don't get the wrong idea. He didn't die or anything. He was one of those astronauts that went to the moon. The one you never heard about, the one they all kept quiet about. It was my grandpa. Went to the moon. A young man. And he liked the moon. And so he decided to live on the moon. (*Trying to keep from laughing and pointing out front*) Got you again, didn't I? My grandpa's alive. Both grandmas and grandpas. It's really my uncle who lives on the moon. (*Laughs*)

My grandma was a singer. Mom's mom, and Grandpa played guitar. That's how they met. Isn't that romantic? Now isn't it? And it's the truth.

My other grandma plays the piano. Grandpa isn't musical though. He collects stamps.

So where was I? Oh, sure. A one and a—Nah! You don't want to see me dance. You want me to recite something? What? What can I recite? I know.
　　(*Very hammy*) "It was many and many a year ago
　　In a kingdom by the sea.
　　There lived a maid whom you may know
　　by the name of . . . Sara Lee?"

Kidding. Just kidding. You see that's my name. Sarah Lee, with an "H." Sarah Lee Walker. (*Parody of a western movie*). So, what do you think about that, pardner?

(*Her normal voice*) Are you just going to let me die up here? I don't mean really die. I mean die like in doing a terrible job, not knowing what to say or do. Or—

I got an idea. I'll tell you about my hobbies. (*Long pause*) I don't have any hobbies. The only thing I'm interested in is being an actress. That's my whole life's ambition. Everything else revolves around that. I'm being serious. I mean it. I know I've been kidding a lot, because, believe it or not, I didn't know what else to do. What else to say. But not now.

Why do people want to be actors or actresses? Why do I want to be an actress? I don't really know. It's just the most wonderful feeling in the world. Everybody watching and listening and the house so still you can hear a hat drop. (*Laughs and points*)—Got you again, didn't I?

(*Serious*) No, but I mean it. It's not like I want to control people, or even that I feel I'm so important or special. (*Pause*) Even though I am. Important and special, I mean. Just kidding. Just kidding.

(*Serious again*) It's like I'm this instrument playing a duet with . . . God maybe? Or the consciousness of the universe. And everything's aligned somehow. And I'm the chemical catalyst or the reed of a tenor sax or the sounding board of a piano. And if I've rehearsed and studied and am confident, well, it's like I'm playing and being played so the audience hears one pure, sweet note. Or a resounding chord.

(*Changing abruptly*) So you heard any good jokes lately?

You'd think with my wanting to perform and loving to be up here on stage that I'd be pretty good at telling jokes. Well, I'm not. I always mess up the punch line. I forget it or something. I wonder why. I can say lines in a play just fine. Right intonation and emphasis. But I can't tell a joke. Maybe life itself's a joke. And we're stuck with one role. I was stuck in one role. A role I hated, till I moved in with Grandma and Grandpa. Can a person be an actress just because her life is—just because she wants to get away, to escape—God, I'm seventeen years old. Why did I want to escape? Why do I still want . . . to . . . escape.

(*An abrupt change*) So, hey, do I have the role or don't I? I mean, I feel like I've been up here forever, and I haven't said a blessed thing. Haven't done a blessed thing. I mean I was always good at ad libbing. When I was in junior high, before I went to the school of performing arts, I joined the speech club. You know, readings and contests and stuff. Well, I always did well with the impromptu event. Give me a subject, and whether I know anything or not about it, I can talk. I'll show you.

Give me a subject, any subject. Say it's . . . quantum physics. All right? Ahem. Ahem. Good evening, ladies and gentlemen.

Quantum physics, huh? What made me think of quantum physics? I don't know what made me think of quantum physics. Black holes. That's it. Quantum physics and black holes.

(*Oratund tones*) Ladies and gentlemen, a discourse on black holes. What is a black hole, ladies and gentlemen? It's a hole in the sky. A hole in the sky that's black. Not brown, not green, not red. But black. Yes, people, it's black. And why is it black? Well, because . . . it isn't really there. It's somewhere else. It's in some other universe. Ha! Didn't think I knew that, did you? A tunnel to the future or the past. Anti-matter.

But you can't go through a black hole. If you tried to go through a black hole, it's hard to tell what would happen besides being crunched down so you'd cover only one billionth of a billionth of a pinhole . . .

So thank you, ladies and gentlemen. My mother thanks you; my father thanks you; my grandmother thanks you; my grandfather thanks you. (*Her voice trails off.*) All of them . . . (*Sadly*) That's dumb. Mom and Dad wouldn't thank . . . But the big thing is that I'll be on my own, and Dad can't—(*Realizing what she's saying*) What am I saying! But if I can play at being someone else, at least for awhile, I really can be that person, become that person, do you see? Everything's better. Everything's different. I'm different. And Dad can't do those things anymore, and Mom can't pretend—(*Panicky*) Oh, my God, I'm sorry. I shouldn't say things like—I'm . . . sorry.

(*Brightly*) So . . . what else would you like to know? (*Pause as if listening to a response*)

I can quit! I really can quit now. And I have the job. Oh, wow, I'll have to tell Grandma and Grandpa. And I'll tell—(*Suddenly, she becomes dignified and composed, a young woman in command of her life*) Thank you. Thank you very much. (*She nods and hurries offstage*)

Questions

1. Why do you suppose Sarah jokes around so much at her audition? Do you think an actor should do that? Why?

2. What feelings is Sarah hiding? Explain. What feelings is she trying to communicate?

3. How true to life is this audition, do you think? Explain.

4. What sorts of things do you think Sarah comes close to saying about her mother and father? Why doesn't she either say what she means or not say anything?

5. What things are illogical in this monologue? Explain. Which are logical? Why do you think she gets the job?

Rupert's Birthday

Ken Jenkins/*U.S.A.*

*R*upert's Birthday, a play complete in itself, is about a woman whose entire life was affected by her helping a cow give birth on the woman's thirteenth birthday. The woman recalls her childhood in this monologue.

If you need to cut the monologue, you might want to skip the first part and begin with the line, "Rupert was born on the same night as my brother, Orville." You can then end with the scene at the slaughterhouse.

THE WOMAN:

Heard it on the news today—183 shopping days left 'til Xmas. Don't mean nothing to me. I don't believe in Santy Claus. Xmas is not my holiday. I don't celebrate Xmas. I don't celebrate any "public works" holidays.

Not Xmas, New Years, Thanksgiving, Easter, Halloween, Valentines', April Fools', nor the Fourth Day of July.

Not Labor Day, Arbor Day, Memorial Day, Flag Day, nor none of the Presidents' birthdays.

Not Mothers' Day, nor Fathers' Day; Not St. Patrick's , St. Mary's, St. Michael's, nor St. Pete's; Not May Day, Dog Day, Groundhog Day, nor Sadie Hawkins' Day.

Not Advent, Pentecost, Good Friday, Ash Wednesday, nor Fat Tuesday; Not the Feasts of the Ascension, the Assumption, the Annunciation, the Apocalypse, nor the Aurora Borealis; Not Passover, Hanukkah, Rosh Hashanah, Candlemas Communion, Holy Incarnation, Transubstantiation, nor the Ides of March.

And—not the Annual Pig Roast and Blue Blood-Letting Contest sponsored by the East Tennessee Chapter of the D.A.R.

Rupert's birthday is my holiday.

Rupert was born on the same night as my brother Orville. I named him. Rupert. Saw the name on a sign in a barbershop. Rupert. Prince Rupert. Looked real distinguished. Had a gleam in his eye.

Rupert outweighed Orville at birth. By about 60 lbs.

Orville was the baby. Seven girls. And then Orville. Seven girls: Francine (who was supposed to have been a boy), Sheila Leigh (who wasn't), Louisa May (that's me), April (born on December 26th), and the triplets, Faith, Hope, and Charity. And then—Orville. Daddy said he almost named him Despair. Faith, Hope, Charity—and Despair. Seven girls: 17, 15, 13 (that's me), 9, 5, 5, and 5. And Mamma thought she was through. And then—Orville. Orville came backwards. Been that way ever since.

Miranda was my "baby." That's what Daddy always said. She was born on my birthday and her real momma died the next day. So I became her "momma." Daddy showed me how to put milk in a rubber glove and then poke a hole in one of the fingers so she could suck on it. Daddy said, "She's your baby now." So I raised her. She got her milk from that old glove twice a day for weeks. I was her "momma" till she died.

Miranda was born in 1955 on my 11th birthday.

Two years later, on my 13th birthday, she gave birth to Rupert.

And on the same night—Momma had Orville.

May 16, 1957. Miranda had Rupert. Momma had Orville. And I got my first period.

Early that morning Daddy had driven down to East Tennessee to look at some farm equipment being sold at public auction and was not expected back until the following day. I had wanted to go with him, but he convinced me that somebody had to stay behind and look after the stock. I was the best with animals. Still am. Francine never cared about them, and Sheila Leigh made them all nervous. April helped me sometimes, though she could never concentrate, and the triplets were just too little to do anything—except get underfoot.

Momma started labor while she was cooking supper. She wasn't at all worried. She'd been through it all before—including triplets—but, we'd all been small babies. Orville weighed 12 lbs. and 8 oz. And—he came out backwards. Or tried to.

Our neighbor, Mrs. Price, who had 8 kids of her own and had been midwife for lots of births, including the triplets, came over to help out, but when she saw how Orville was trying to come out, she called Doc Fisher who said, "Bring her to the hospital! Right now!"

So, Mr. Price came over in his station wagon and drove Momma the 14 miles into town to the hospital.

Francine went with them.

Sheila Leigh was having hysterics from all the excitement and finally passed out on the living room couch. I just threw a quilt on her and let her be.

Then I read a story to April and the girls and they went right off to sleep.

I was still wide awake, so I went outside and stood in the middle of the front yard and stared up at the man-in-the-moon. "Mr. Moon," I said, "You look after my Momma. We need her around here." I held my face up to the sky, my head tilted way back—like this—and said, "Please, Mr. Moon. We really do need her."

I listened. The moon didn't answer.

What I heard was: an old hen squawking as she fell off the roost, the creak of the front porch swing, coon dogs barking somewhere off in the woods, and Miranda mooing.

She was standing in a pool of moonlight looking very regal. And very pregnant. She was due in June. Or so we thought.

She mooed again and turned and walked into the barn.

"You smart aleck," I thought, "you've got no business in there." Someone, me probably, had forgotten to latch the gate.

Well, I started to cross the yard to go get her and all of a sudden my head got light and my knees gave out, and I saw the ground come floating up to hit me in the face.

I passed out.

When I came to, I was lying on my back in the front yard looking straight up at the full moon. I felt like I was floating. Being held up by the moon.

Then I saw the blood.

I had started my first period.

I looked down at the dark stain in the center of my clean white nightgown, and I thought of Momma lying on her back on a clean, white sheet with a child struggling to come out through the center of her body.

"Momma and I are both bleeding tonight. I am helping Momma birth that baby. I and the moon. We are helping Momma."

Then I heard Miranda again. She was grunting and groaning as if *she* were in labor.

"Miranda's helping Momma, too," was my first thought. My second thought was, "That's impossible. She's not due 'til June."

I primed the pump and filled a basin with cold water from the well and washed the blood from myself and from my nightgown and hung my nightgown up in the branches of a white ash tree.

And there I stood.

Hard brown body in the silver light of a bright full moon shivering with chill bumps and looking in some wonder at my "new" body.

"This is a woman's body now," I thought, "the blood that has flowed from me tonight has united me for all time to every woman who has ever walked the earth."

"And you've seen it all, haven't you, Mr. Moon."

Miranda groaned again. "She can't be in labor. She's not due 'til June." Or so we thought.

Barefoot and jaybird naked I tiptoed across the white graveled driveway and stood by the barn door.

The wet pump handle sparkled in the moonlight.

My nightgown fluttered in the green leaves of the white ash tree.

"That nightgown belongs to Louisa May the Girl," I thought, "I am Louisa May the Woman now. I need a new nightgown."

Miranda was standing in the small lot in back of the barn where she'd been born two years before. My "baby" Miranda.

"Well, what about it?" I said.

She looked at me and switched her tail, and shook her ears, and bobbed her head up and down, and turned around so I could see her backside.

And there, glistening in the moonlight, were two little feet sticking out about three inches from her swollen vulva.

"For crying out loud, Miranda, you're not supposed to be having that baby *now!* You're not due 'til June!"

Or so we thought.

Miranda lifted her tail, shifted her weight back and forth on her hind legs, and arched her back in a contraction that pushed the calf's feet out of her body clear up to its knees. They were front feet. That was good. At least the calf was going to come out frontwards. Unlike dumb Orville who was trying to come out backside first.

"Oh, my god! Momma! I forgot all about Momma!"

"Well, I can't do anything about Momma. But, I can do something about this."

So I climbed up into the loft and threw down the brightest bale of straw I could find and spread it out in a corner of the lot out of the draft.

Miranda walked over to it, gave it a sniff or two, and lay right down and commenced to have another huge contraction.

The calf's nose had already appeared. I could see its blue tongue spilling over its chin where it rested on the front legs. In good position. Not breathing yet. Not using air. Still attached to its Momma. Breathing through her blood.

I thought, "What if I have to pull it?"

I had watched calves come before, and once or twice I had seen Daddy pull them when the cow was having trouble.

In my mind's eye I saw Daddy's strong hands and arms clasp the slippery legs of the calf and pull out and down, in rhythm with the cow's contractions, until the head and shoulders of the calf were through the narrow opening of the cervix.

I looked down at my own small hands and thought, "These are no good. But if push comes to shove, I'll try. I'll have to. I'm the one that's here."

I watched Miranda closely for about an hour, stayed right by her side. She'd get up and walk around, and then she'd lay back down and have another series of contractions. And every time she'd get to the point where the broad part of the calf's forehead would almost clear the cervix, she wouldn't be able to get it out any farther. And she would stop pushing, and the calf would slip back inside her womb.

Cows are real strong, but the birthing muscles will wear out, and if the cervix doesn't stretch enough to let the calf through before the cow's muscles are too weak to push, then the cow will quit trying . . . and the calf will die inside her womb. Eventually the cow will die, too.

Well, I was just beginning to realize that I was really going to have to do something when Miranda turned to me and seemed to say, "C'mon you big dummy! I need some help! What are you waiting on? Xmas!"

So, the next time she lay down, I took a couple of burlap feed sacks and got right up close behind her.

She was lying on her right side, with her legs sticking out—like this.

I lay down on my right side, facing her rear end—like this.

Then, I coiled up like a spring, with my knees bent up, and my bare feet flush against the muscles of her back legs.

Then, I wrapped a feed sack around each of the calf's front legs and tied them on with double strands of baling twine.

Then, I looped the strands of twine together between the calf's legs so that there was just enough room for my two hands to grab a hold of. I got a firm hold and waited.

When Miranda pushed—I pulled.

I pulled for all that I was worth.

Every time she'd get the calf's head up in place, she'd have to stop and rest. And every time she'd stop pushing, the calf would start slipping back inside her.

"C'mon, Miranda, you can do it."

After several series of contractions I was dripping with sweat, and every muscle in my body felt like it was on fire.

"It's now or never, Miranda, you hear? I ain't got much more strength left in me."

She pushed—and I pulled. I held my breath and pulled with all my might. I stretched my body taut like a bow string.

"C'mon, Miranda!"

And just when I thought I was going to explode, Miranda gave a great groan, and out sloshed the calf's head and shoulders and slid right up my naked body and came to rest with its head lying in my lap.

Its body and back legs were still inside Miranda. Umbilical still attached. Half in Miranda—and half lying on top of me.

I looked at the calf's head lying there, wet, between my legs: not yet quite alive, blue tongue lolling sideways out of its mouth, nose still full of birth, ears slicked back against its head, eyes dull and lifeless.

And—as I was looking at the calf's eye—Miranda stood up.

And, as she stood, the rest of the calf's body slipped out, and—the umbilical broke.

And—as the umbilical broke—a *light* switched on in that calf's eye!

I saw it!

It came to life! Life came to it.

As the umbilical broke—it became itself.

It became conscious. It saw.

And the first thing that it saw—was me. Me—looking right at it. Looking right in at it.

I saw the first flash of life come into that calf's eye. Saw it switch on—like a light in a dark room.

It was a bull calf. Dark red with a white star on his forehead. Big framey calf. Distinguished looking.

Well, I stayed there with Miranda and her baby until she'd cleaned him up, and coaxed him up on all four wobbly legs, and helped him find the udder, and he had sucked the first rich colostrum milk, and was ready for a nap, and then I got some soap and a towel and went swimming in the pond.

Floating on my back in the deep water I looked up at the moon and said, "Everything's O.K. on this end, Mr. Moon. I just hope you're taking care of Momma."

The moon did the best he could.

What happened was—Doc Fisher had to open Momma's stomach with a knife and reach in and pull Orville out by the ears. 12 lb. and 8 oz. And tried to come out backwards.

Momma was wore out for a while.

Orville was fine.

May 16, 1957.

Momma had Orville—with no help from him. Miranda had Rupert—with a little help from me.

May 16, 1957.

I turned 13. And my Daddy brought me home a store-bought dolly from East Tennessee for my birthday. I was happy to get it—but, I laughed to myself to think that I was a "woman" now—and here I was—playing with a dolly dressed in a white nightgown trimmed with blue ribbon and white lace.

The next day I made myself a new nightgown. Patterned it after this dolly's dress. First thing I'd ever sewed in my life . . . all by myself. White cotton trimmed with blue ribbons and white lace.

Every year I make myself a new nightgown. White cotton. Blue ribbons. White lace.

(She puts on the gown)

Momma and Daddy have long since passed away.

My sisters are all scattered to the winds. Some married. Some not. Some with children. Some not. They all write. And come to "visit" on "holidays."

Orville runs a gas station in town. He comes out. Sometimes. We talk.

May 16, 1958.

Exactly one year after Orville and Rupert were born. I was 14.

May 16, 1958.

Rupert's birthday.

Daddy and I loaded Rupert into the truck and carried him into town to be slaughtered for meat.

I didn't cry.

I rode in the back with Rupert and held his huge head in my arms and thought, "One year ago today this big, old head was so small that it could fit between my legs."

At the slaughterhouse I made Daddy and the butcher be real quiet while I stood in the killing chute with Rupert and rubbed his belly and scratched his neck until he relaxed and lifted up his head and looked me in the eye.

Then, when he was calm and happy, I nodded at the butcher and he shot him in the back of the head. Shot him clean.

He died instantly.

I was looking right in Rupert's eye when the gun went off—and—I saw the light go out in his eye.

I saw it.

I saw the light flash on when he was born. I saw it go out when he was killed.

I was 14.

My sisters all think I'm crazy. I don't send Xmas nor Easter cards. I don't know when any of their children were born. I don't go to church . . . the days of the week are all the same to me. I'm not afraid of dying . . . and I'm not tired of living.

I live alone out here on the old home place. And the days of celebration in other peoples' lives means little, or nothing, to me.

Orville understands. Big dummy that he is. Orville understands.

I do not celebrate "public works" holidays.

(*The doll rocks in the chair*)

Not Xmas, New Years, Thanksgiving, Easter, Halloween, Valentines', April Fools', not the Fourth Day of July.

(*Lights begin to fade*)

Not Labor Day, Arbor Day, Memorial Day, Flag Day, nor none of the Presidents' birthdays.

(*Lights to half*)

Not Mothers' Day, nor Fathers' Day, nor May Day, Dog Day, Groundhog Day, Derby Day . . .

(*Lights to black*)

. . . nor Sadie Hawkins' Day.

Questions

1. Why is Rupert's birthday so important to the woman? Explain.

2. Why does the woman not celebrate any holidays or even go to church? Is it logical that she would let herself be so affected by what happened in the story she tells?

3. Is there any significance to her continuing to live at the home place? Explain.

4. What emotions do you think the woman felt when Rupert was slaughtered? Why?

5. Do you find this monologue true-to-life or believable? Why?

Playing time: One minute and 30 seconds to
one minute 50 seconds
Character's age: 18 to 20

FOB

David Henry Hwang/ *U.S.A.*

This play is from *Broken Promises: Four Plays by David Henry Hwang,* in which the author says that the included plays are his "attempt to explore human issues without denying the color of my skin."

The title means "fresh off the boat," referring to new immigrants. Two of the three characters, Steve and Grace, move between being themselves and being fictional Chinese warriors, who were created, according to Hwang, by "two figures from American literature." These two writers are Maxine Hong Kingston and Frank Chin.

Grace is a college student attending UCLA. In this monologue, she is explaining how difficult it is to be a person of Chinese heritage living in America. She feels she can be neither Chinese nor American.

GRACE:

Yeah. It's tough trying to live in Chinatown. But it's tough trying to live in Torrance, too. It's true. I don't like being alone. You know, when Mom could finally bring me to the U.S., I was already ten. But I never studied my English very hard in Taiwan, so I got moved back to the second grade. There were a few Chinese girls in the fourth grade, but they were American-born, so they wouldn't even talk to me. They'd just stay with themselves and compare how much clothes they all had, and make fun of the way we all talked. I figured I had a better chance of getting in with the white kids than with them, so in junior high I started bleaching my hair and hanging out at the beach—you know, Chinese hair looks pretty lousy when you bleach it. After a while, I knew what beach was gonna be good on any given day, and I could tell who was coming just by his van. But the American-born Chinese, it didn't matter to them. They just giggled and went to their own dances. Until my senior year in high school— that's how long it took for me to get over this whole thing. One night I took Dad's car and drove on Hollywood Boulevard, all the way from downtown to Beverly Hills, then back on Sunset. I was looking and listening—all the time with the window down, just so I'd feel like I was part of the city. And that Friday, it was—I guess—I said, "I'm lonely. And I don't like it. I don't like being alone." And that was all. As soon as I said it, I felt all of the breeze—it was really cool on my face—and I heard all of the radio—and the music sounded really good, you know? So I drove home.

Questions

1. Why do you think Grace for a time tried to be white? Can you empathize with her in doing that? Do you think she should deny her Chinese heritage?

2. Can you see the significance of the title in this monologue? Explain.

3. What purpose did the drive in the car serve for Grace? What did she get out of it?

4. How do you think Grace felt when she first was enrolled in an American school?

5. Why does Grace say it's tough to live both in Chinatown and Torrance?

Playing time: Five minutes and 15 seconds to
five minutes and 45 seconds
Character's age: 18 to 22

American Tropical

Richard Ford/ *U.S.A.*

American Tropical is essentially a one-person play, although other characters appear with a few lines.

Throughout the piece, Evelyn, the central character, is
explaining how she killed someone whom she caught with
her boyfriend and how she feels about the killing.

According to the playwright, Evelyn is in her late teens or
early twenties, though she acts older. The scene takes place
in a trailer park in central Florida.

EVELYN:

(*Abstracted.*) Sometimes we take the short view too much, I think. I used to hope to teach civics someday. That was my best subject at Wyandotte. The Bill of Rights. The Magna Charta. All that. But now I never will because I'm not civic enough myself. The older I get, the more the facts of life are clear to me, I know I'll never teach civics. That's a fact, even though I have experience others don't and I think I have goodwill toward everyone.

[SID (*Smiling.*) That's what everyone thinks.]

EVELYN (*Ignoring him.*) People will talk to you down here in the tropics. A man over there (*Points offstage.*) told me that when they were starting *Candid Camera* they tried to start in Michigan. But no one would talk to them. So they came to Florida. And that's why so many of them had Southerners' accents. I don't know what I'd do if people didn't talk to me now. My ears are humming all the time, and it's better when people are talking, or even when I'm talking. I know I lie in bed at night and watch the little window on the clock. Watch the numbers flip down, sometimes all night long. And my ears will be humming, humming. I should go have tests made, though I know well enough what I'm suffering from.

(*Suzie leaves the table and comes to Evelyn and whispers, then waits for an answer.*)

EVELYN Yes, sweetheart. You certainly may.

(*Suzie turns and runs toward the mobile home, making a sashay skip past her father, who has turned now to watch Evelyn, smiling in admiration of her. Evelyn takes a drink of her beer.*)

EVELYN I wish I didn't drink these. But I do. (*Pause*) I always thought kidnapping was the stupidest of crimes. I never knew why anybody'd get interested in it. You always get caught. But at least the *person* gets away, or has the chance to. But killing. *That's* the stupidest crime of them all. Way past kidnapping and the rest. Wyandotte is close to Detroit, so you have a chance to think about it all while you're growing up. I think with killing, apart from the thing itself, the worst is that you *seem* to get away. But no one really goes free.

[SID (*From the table.*) She's not really mean. Sometimes women just don't have characters where other women are concerned. It's funny. (*Smiles in wonder.*) My first wife was like that. Exactly the same.]

EVELYN I hear God, I think. I saw in a newspaper the other day, it was the *Pennysaver*. I saw a ticket advertised for Holy Rome. Somebody had bought a tour ticket, then couldn't go for some reason at the last minute and was stuck. I thought to myself: Take it. When am I going to see Rome? It's a holy place, and I'm Catholic. See Rome and Die was going to be my motto on the trip.

(*Sid leaves the table and comes to the chair beside Evelyn and whispers something to her, then laughs softly, as if it was a private joke between them.*)

EVELYN (*To Sid.*) You think I'm a fool? Don't think that, because you'd be wrong.

(*Sid laughs good-naturedly, then bends and kisses her on the cheek.*)

[SID (*To audience.*) She's a genius, really, isn't she? (*Sid walks away toward the mobile home, climbs the steps and passes Suzie coming back out. Suzie carries a jar of cold cream in her hands. She heads for Evelyn.*)]

EVELYN I read someplace on the way down here about a woman with a brain tumor. They operated on her and took eighty percent of her subconscious mind. She can still walk and talk and think, in a way. She just doesn't keep things much anymore. I thought—seriously—that wouldn't be so bad. Women have characters, no matter what he thinks about the subject. (*Motions at trailer and Sid.*) People always like to say it's hard for us to know what we think about things. But I know what I think. And what I think about myself. My mother taught me not to kill another person. And now I've done that in Michigan.

(*Suzie sits on the ground at Evelyn's feet in a posture of apparent adoration. She uncaps the cold cream and begins carefully to rub it into Evelyn's legs, using her hands.*)

EVELYN That's nice, Suzie. That's very nice.

(*Light is almost down. The spot illuminates Evelyn and Suzie. Evelyn gazes up into the dark sky.*)

EVELYN We'll probably get new weather now. That'll make me dizzy. Weather's the only part of Michigan I can honestly say I don't miss, the only part I won't be glad to see when I go back to enter prison.

(*Suzie looks at her strangely, as if each of them is in a trance. Evelyn smokes her cigarette, blows smoke into the darkness.*)

EVELYN (*Conversationally.*) I've always put my faith in men. Maybe that was a mistake and I'll live to regret it. Maybe I'm living that regret right now and have nothing but misery to look forward to. Love is just a loss, isn't it? (*Pause.*) What's the use of making a hunted criminal of yourself? That's a good argument, one I could listen to if I could hear anything but a hum that I'm sure is not just the weather changing and that will only get louder. I wish my friend Penny had said that. But.

(*Suzie stops applying the cold cream and screws the top back on the jar, then sits back, staring at Evelyn.*)

EVELYN I've never disliked being an adult. Never wished I was a young girl again. Yet you feel yourself to be in a position which is the very one you didn't want to be in. That is, come to a bad end. And you can feel like a child about it and wish you could be a child and get out of it. Though that's not so easy anymore, either. I've wished I had my own virginity back more than once in the last month. Sometimes you just start out to do something, and then something else happens. You know? Only you've caused it.

(*Evelyn caresses Suzie's hair. Suzie puts her head on Evelyn's knee, while Evelyn continues soothing her. A light goes on in the dark trailer.*)

EVELYN Illusion is not my adversary. Definitely. Even though I'm adaptable. Sid has said I'm a clear thinker and hopeful. But I have to go to the phones in a pretty little bit of time now. We need to have good experiences so our memories can be sweet. And we can't live forever. Though it's too bad my family isn't famous; then I could write about what I've done, and people would love it, and somebody'd get rich.

(*The porch light goes on at the mobile home. The door opens. Sid comes to the screen, look out silently into the dark. Evelyn pats Suzie to rouse her. Suzie collects the items on the ground and stands.*)

EVELYN (*Softly to Suzie.*) Take this, sweetheart.

(*Evelyn gives Suzie the beer bottle. Suzie walks slowly to the mobile home. She enters past her father, who remains at the door watching Evelyn, who stands, holding her cigarettes and ashtray.*)

EVELYN Other people don't make you happy or unhappy. You do it all by yourself. Right? So, maybe I've been wrong in putting my faith in men and doing things like killing a girl out of passion. I know eyes are important to me. I have always trusted people or not due to their eyes. My best friends have trusting eyes. And then one of them wasn't so much. (*Pause.*) So what can you do if you're me? I've always had the feeling of sailing before the storm. And now the storm has caught up with me and all around. (*Pause.*) Just-as-long-as-you're-happy-then-to-hell-with-the-rest is not an especially good motto. I cried when my father died, I know that. (*Shakes her head in wonder.*) What keeps us all from crime I don't know.

(*She turns toward the mobile home, walks toward it, climbs the steps, enters past where Sid is standing.*)

Questions

1. What sorts of feelings does Evelyn have about killing Penny? How do you know?

2. What do you think is the main point the playwright is trying to make here? Explain.

3. Other than being a killer, what type of person is Evelyn? Why does she act older than she is? Describe her as best you can.

4. Evelyn regrets the killing for a number of reasons. What are they?

5. What do you think will happen to Evelyn? What should happen? Why?

Playing time: Thirteen to fourteen minutes
Character's age: 17 to 18

Steps

Susan Vreeland/ *U.S.A.*

This piece is complete in itself, and tells the poignant tale of a friendship between a girl and a boy that has lasted through most of their school years. But now it's graduation night, and each will be going separate ways.

Susan Vreeland is the author of many published stories and a biographical novel, *What Love Sees.* She teaches both ceramics and high school honors classes in English and is also a well-known travel writer.

If this monologue needs to be shortened, you can begin with the words "Even in elementary school" at the beginning of the fourth paragraph. You can end with: "He picked up his bike and rode away, his front wheel wobbling across the dirt playground."

THE NARRATOR:

It's graduation night, a big party's going on—the end of everything because pretty soon we'll go off to different colleges—and I'm sitting in the dark on the stairs of my old elementary school. Alone. I move under the floodlight so Torin can see me, the circle of yellow around my skirt like a spotlight. If he comes soon, I won't miss everything. The grad night party's pretty important—a way to finish it off, put all that teenage stuff behind us. I keep checking my watch every ten minutes.

Torin didn't graduate. He failed two classes because he never handed in homework even though he aced the tests. He had to turn down his scholarship to Art Students League in New York, so he's leaving town tomorrow for a job with some art guy he met at a comic book convention.

He was pretty serious when he asked me to meet him. "After dark at the corner of Bixby and Grandview, alone," he says like it's some kind of drug deal. As if he has to give me directions. He's different that way, precise when he doesn't need to be.

Even in elementary school, Torin was different, not just because of his hair so blond it blinded you or because he always played Vikings instead of kickball. The day I met him, we're all eating peanut butter and jelly sandwiches from our lunch pails and he pulls out a tin of sardines. And then he wiggles one in front of my face and slurps it down. I think we became friends because I didn't squeal like the other girls did.

He was the only guy I knew that had such oddball stuff in his room. Instead of Star Trek posters, he had these drawings where stairways go weird around a building and never get anywhere. He put duct tape on the carpet to mark the part of the room where he allowed his mother and grandparents to go. And on his dresser in a shoebox, lying on a bunch of Kleenex, was this stone chin. His uncle stole it off a Greek statue in Ephesus. Wherever. "But I like the Norse gods better than the Greek," Torin says, like some kind of a professor. "They aren't so perfect, and they do things without knowing why." Geezus, I didn't know anything about any gods.

We were a strange pair, I suppose. He'd come and scrape on my bedroom window at midnight to get me to sneak out for some secret mission. Once it was to sew the legs of his new jeans closed, fill them with rocks, and race around the neighborhood on our bikes dragging them on a rope so they'd get the right used look.

Another time we made crossbows out of two rulers that could shoot potato pellets at people's windows, and in the middle of the night he came over with a wad of black cloth. "Look what I got," he says like it's a hundred dollar bill or something.

"What is it?"

"Judy's old dance tights." He always called his mom Judy, as if she were a real human being and not just his mom.

"What do we need them for?"

He takes out his pocket knife. "One leg for each of us, with eye holes. It's no fun if potato pellet targets know who you are."

I suppose we were all pretty different. That was Mrs. Hoffstetter's fault, if you call it fault. In the fifth grade we were in this special gifted class, Global Culture, and we were doing this opera. All right, we were only lip-synching the words but we were doing *Aida* in Italian. Not even something kiddie like *Peter and the Wolf.* She taught us a little Italian like excuse me how do you get to the Colosseum and we learned about opera stories and Verdi, and she took us downtown to see *Rigoletto* about a hunchback. We learned about Egyptian tombs and chariots and Tutankhamen because Aida is Egyptian. We painted sets with pyramids and temples, and made costumes and practiced the songs, our chests out and our arms waving. It was the biggest thing in our lives, and Torin's mom was the choreographer. I knew that was a big deal for him because she wasn't the type of PTA lady other mothers were. She was a dancer, and I'd seen men in leather coming to their house to pick her up on motorcycles.

Judy was beautiful, tall and thin with white blond hair pulled back tight in a knot, so from the front it hardly seemed like she had any hair and you just looked at her face more. She danced with us, not just calling out the steps like a teacher. When we did the back side front hop slide for the ritual dance of the priests and priestesses, she sort of sang it to us, her voice and her body going deep on the slide and so far sideways that she was halfway across the room already. "Get a lot out of your slide," she said. "Get a lot out of everything," and her smile had a brightness that made us dance.

And when she did the stomp kick for the triumphal march, her leg shot straight over our heads. "That's it, kick!" she said and we kicked because she sang it out so that the kick was the most natural thing to do.

After a while she stopped coming and we just practiced what we had already learned.

"Why hadn't Judy been here?" I asked at recess. "*Aida's* only a couple weeks from now."

"She has a brain tumor," Torin said and I thought he was kidding, but then he was absent for a week, and one day Mrs. Hoffstetter said, "Torin's coming back tomorrow. We should all be kind to him. His mother died."

I choked on my gum. The class closed up real quiet and just stared down at their desks. Who would buy his sardines, I wondered. He didn't have a dad. It didn't occur to me right that minute that his grandparents lived in the same house.

I raised my hand. "Is he still going to sit way over there?" I asked. It was no fun having him away from the rest of the class in a puny desk by the wall, but he pinched people and ripped their homework so Mrs. Hoffstetter slapped him with the worst—punishment by separation.

"We'll see. We'll see how he acts."

That was what I was afraid of. I thought he'd be a puffy-faced mopey guy with red watery eyes. Maybe wearing a black T-shirt. I was afraid he wouldn't scrape on my bedroom window at night anymore. But when he came back he was the same skinny weird kid as before. He still ate those slimy sardines and he still wore his favorite red shirt with the purple dragon. And at recess we still played Vikings.

During arithmetic, I watched him draw the Temple of Vulcan on his long division paper. He usually drew Viking ships with carved beaks or something else no one but him knew anything about—like Pluto's helmet or that giant fork thing of Poseidon. His favorite was Thor's hammer, because of his name and all, but this time it was the Temple of Vulcan with Radames' and Aida's tomb underneath, all cold and clammy looking, with the priests and priestesses dancing above it, and above the dancers, their names. He put my name right next to his with a single underline under both of them. I had a feeling that if he was drawing the other things, Mrs. Hoffstetter would make him stop like she always did.

After lunch that day, we practiced the steps Judy taught us as far as we knew them while Mrs. Hoffstetter worked with the leads on the arias. Torin was doing the back side front hop slide for the ritual dance, and his face looked as though his mind was on Mars. He danced like a great, dark bird, his arms lifting slowly and holding him up so that his feet hardly touched the floor until the slide. When he started to show us what Judy was going to teach us next, the second half of the stomp kick pattern for the triumphal march, Mrs. Hoffstetter brought over another lady, Mrs. Schart, and introduced her as the new dancing teacher. With Mrs. Hoffstetter standing at her side nodding like a maniac, Mrs. Schart announced that the steps would be changed.

I looked at Torin. He was stuck in position, with one knee raised, ready to stomp. His eyes drilled into her. I had a flash that some bigtime crime was being committed.

"Why can't we do it the way it was?" I asked.

"We think it will be easier," Mrs. Hoffstetter said, and that was that.

Instead of the back side front hop slide, we were told to do a stupid step together step for the ritual dance. And for the triumphal fanfare, the stomp kick pattern was changed to just marching in place. And the slave dance was shortened to just what we'd learned.

"We still get to do crack-the-whip for the victory celebration, don't we?" I asked.

"Yes."

In the rehearsal, Torin was quiet. He danced the new steps but he looked like one of the soldiers instead of the priest he was supposed to be.

The weeks after that, all he drew was Thor's hammer. He called it Mjolnir and said it was a powerful weapon that Thor could throw, hit somebody and it would come back into his hand to throw again. And his pictures of Thor changed, too. He made him into a bad guy with eyes like slits and pointy ears as if the wind was blowing the skin of his face back. He invited me over to hear his new tapes. They were by a group I hadn't heard of before—The Dead Kennedys. "Judy's boyfriend gave them to me," he said.

I didn't understand it then, but now I see that something went different in him. He did start dressing in black like the older punk guys from the junior high did, and it didn't mean mourning. Exactly. And he bought these mean looking, too big combat boots with some money the boyfriend gave him. He had a kind of a turning.

The night of the performance was the first time we got to look at the program. At the bottom it said: "The students in Mrs. Hoffstetter's Fifth Grade Class are all grateful for the loving assistance of Mrs. Judy Hill, choreographer, who passed away March something-or-other." I saved mine for a long time.

Nobody waved to his parents in the audience or acted silly. The music, louder than we were allowed to play it during rehearsals, swirled around us and all there was was the palace and the costumes and the voices and the temple. We felt pretty cool because we knew we were doing something well that we weren't even supposed to like.

The best part was crack-the-whip during the victory celebration. We were all holding hands whirling around and Torin was on the end and I was next to him. The chorus belted out "Gloria al Egitto," and the line of arms curved faster and faster, whipping us at the end, and when the music got loudest I heard Torin's voice, "Let go of my hand," and when I did he went flying off across the stage into the orchestra pit and the audience gasped and I heard Mrs. Hoffstetter backstage say, "Torin!" and I knew he was loving it. Trying not to smile, he stood up on the steps to the stage and bowed low like he had a stick in his back, and the audience applauded.

That night after the performance, I followed Mom around the house while she got ready for bed and pestered her with questions about whether she ever danced or sang or played piano or painted or carved statues or did something like that. I think I wanted to sleep with her that night like when I was little, but knew I was too old.

Good thing because after a while I heard Torin scratching at my bedroom window. Outside, he didn't say anything, just got on his bike. I followed him to school, and we wedged our bikes through the playground gate where the chain was long, went up to the auditorium where the floodlight lit up the steps, then went around to the back where the transom window into the boy's bathroom was open. "How'd you know?" I asked.

"I opened it," he said, like it was only obvious. From his jacket, he pulled out a rope with loops knotted in it and a handle of a garden hoe tied at one end and threw it so it caught in the V of the open window. "Who first?"

"You," I whispered, but I followed right after. Inside, we stood still for a minute and there was only silent, dark space, like the inside of a pyramid. It even smelled like a tomb, musty and cold. We stumbled around, suffocating, our steps echoing, until Torin switched on a blue stage light. We could see only the painted stone wall of Radames' and Aida's tomb and the first two rows of seats. The place seemed hollow, different than when it was full of people.

Torin didn't look at me, just hummed the music, and started, back side front hop. Then he just stood there, stiff. He tried with the other foot, back side front hop.

"Can't remember. Can't you remember? The steps."

I started, back side front hop, and then my mind blanked. I felt him watching me so I started again. Nothing.

He tried the stomp kick pattern, then froze. I kicked too, but then forgot what came after the kick—just the marching in place pounded in my head. My toes hurt from trying to squeeze out the steps, but they weren't there.

He stared at his feet a long time, then looked out to the black auditorium, as if the answer would come from an empty seat. "Can't remember," he said so softly I barely heard him, turned off the lights and we climbed out. When he walked through the yellow circle of the floodlight, his face glistened. He picked up his bike and rode away, his front wheel wobbling across the dirt playground.

I didn't see him for two days after the opera. When he came to school on Monday, he had shaved his head.

He gave my mom the Temple of Vulcan drawing with the tomb underneath, and she put it on the refrigerator. After that he brought her other drawings and always asked her if he was getting any better, even though he'd give this crooked smile that meant he knew he was. We came into the kitchen one day from junior high and I said "Hi Mom," and I heard him say "Hi Mom" behind me.

A month ago I heard him ask her for a recipe for chicken a l'orange, and when I went over to his house last week she asked me to get the crepe maker from him. "He borrowed it to make breakfast in bed for someone," she said, like stupid me for not knowing.

I know Mom would understand why I'm not going to the party even if my friends don't, why I'll wait for him all night here on the steps 'til he comes. I have to make sure he'll be all right even though he didn't get to graduate and won't be at the party. Naturally he'd want to meet me at night. The day always seemed too small for him. The party's hopping by now, but I try not to think of it, that it's our last night together. After a while I hear footsteps and spin around.

"I knew you'd know I wanted to meet you right here. Let's try to get in," Torin says, but the transom is closed, so we just sit on the steps and look out across the dark playground, trying to imagine what's ahead. We say a little about the years and our midnight adventures, but mostly we just think. The end of high school stops all that for good, and the weight of its closing feels heavy.

"They didn't let me see Judy in the hospital," he says right out of the blue, "so I never got to say goodbye, but one time she told me that except in dance, endings weren't as important as beginnings."

Torin stands up and I think he wants to go, but when I look up at him, he's moving his feet—back side front hop, and then, slowly, stretching it out, he does a deep slide. His face stretches into a grin, and he does it on the other foot, back side front hop slide, and the slide goes forever, and I know it's wrong but I jump up and do it with him, back side front hop slide, over and over, our slides getting longer and longer, and we're singing the steps and they're not right but he thinks they are, and then he sings out "Gloria al Egitto" and we hold hands and swing around in a circle of light like in the triumphal celebration until we collapse into each other on the steps.

Under the floodlight, our chests beating against each other's, I ask, "How'd you remember?"

"It just came to me. I wasn't even trying." He shrugs. "I wanted you to know."

We walk down the steps and across the playground, the Gloria echoing in my mind, and I know I am too full for any party.

Questions

1. Why is it so important for the narrator to meet with Torin before going to the party?

2. Why do you think the narrator and Torin are such good friends?

3. The narrator says that Torin did a lot of weird things. Why do you think he did them? Did the narrator think he was a weird person? Explain.

4. How do you think the narrator feels about going away and leaving Torin?

5. What sorts of feelings do you think the narrator has for Torin? How do you think he feels about her? Why?

Monologues
for Males

Sounding Brass

Marsh Cassady/ *U.S.A.*

Sounding Brass is the story of a young man's growing up in the coal mining regions of Pennsylvania in the 1940s and 1950s. It follows him from the age of about ten or eleven on up through his college years.

In this scene, Martin is talking with his best friend Frank, who thinks it is strange that Martin never mentioned his folks. This scene explains why.

MARTIN:

You wonder why I never mentioned my folks. Okay, Frank, I'll tell you. They never wanted me. I was an unwelcome intruder, stealing pieces of their lives. I remember one time when I was a little kid, my mother accused me of trying to kill her by being born and of ruining her career as a musician. She said that every time she tried to practice, I cried. "You were a selfish little boy," she said. And another time when I was no more than three or four, she packed her suitcase and said she was leaving and not coming back. I was such a horrible child, she said, that I didn't deserve a mother. She left, and I was all alone with no one to care how hard I cried. (*Exhales sharply*) I wasn't allowed to call them Mom and Dad. They were Helen and Dan to me and everyone else. (*Pause*) You know, he was just as bad as she was, maybe even worse.

When I was fifteen, just before Christmas in 1954, my sophomore year in high school, my grandparents came for a visit. Grandpa and I were sitting at the kitchen table talking about some evangelist or other, Billy Graham, I think. Anyhow, I said he was rich and should use all that money to help the poor. Grandpa disagreed, and I asked him to explain what he meant. Dan was sitting in a chair up against the wall off to one side repairing a toaster or something. He told me to stop arguing, and I said we weren't; we were just talking. I turned back and started to say something else to Grandpa. Dan jumped up and grabbed my arm and dragged me into the dining room.

A powerful man, a good three inches shorter than I was, still he outweighed me. I tried to struggle free, but he slammed me into a corner, grabbed me around the neck and began to squeeze. At the same time he pounded my head—crack! crack! crack!—against the wall. Stop, I thought, oh, God, please stop! He'd hurt me before, but never like this. (*Swallows*)

My vision began to go like a gate being shut across my eyes, starting at the periphery and swinging in toward the center. I grabbed Dan's wrists and tried to pry his hands from around my neck. He only squeezed harder. Helen was upstairs making up a bed for Grandma and Grandpa and must have heard the commotion. She came tearing down and into the dining room. "Dan!" she screamed running toward him and grabbing his arm. "Stop, for God's sake, stop! You're going to kill him."

He released me then and stepped back. I staggered forward and caught my balance. It felt like my throat was crushed, and there was this ring of white hot fire around my neck. I raced to the kitchen, grabbed my coat from a hook by the door, shrugged into it, and stumbled outside and down the steps of the porch.

The night was clear and cold; I was supposed to go caroling in Clivesville. I zipped up my jacket, ran down Second and turned up the hill. By the time I got to Sixth, I had the worst headache of my life, so bad it was making me ill. I slowed to a walk. (*Pause*)

I knew my father was frustrated; I knew money was scarce. Most of the kids who took music lessons had quit because their parents couldn't afford to pay him. But that wasn't my fault, damn it. My dad didn't need to take it out on me. As I was thinking these things, I stopped for a moment, aware of the utter silence. No sound at all, not even the barking of a dog. I started trudging on again, the blades of grass at the side of the road breaking under my feet like thin glass. I knew I couldn't go caroling now, but I kept on walking toward Clivesville.

My jacket had a fur collar; an aviator's jacket, maroon in color, and that soft fur rubbed my neck so bad I could hardly stand it. I un-zipped the jacket and took it off. So what if I got sick? The wind whipped through the neck of my shirt like icy water rolling down my back. What was I going to do when I got to Clivesville? I thought. What did it matter? Nobody cared; I wasn't sure I cared myself. I thought: my father always treats me like I was worthless—my mother too. So maybe I am worthless. And I thought maybe I'd freeze to death and that would be that. Or I'd get hit by a car. Maybe I'd try to help things along.

I fluffed my jacket into a pillow and laid it on the white center line of that macadam road, old Route 30, the Lincoln Highway. So I lay down, my head in the middle of the jacket, and drew my legs up to my chest and closed my eyes. I figured if I were lucky, it would all end quickly. But nothing happened.

After awhile I opened my eyes. My breath hung in the air like a trail of ghostly balloons. Occasionally, a leaf blew by, or I heard a far-off car horn. I began to shake. The running and the walking had made me sweat, and the sweat was beginning to freeze. Time passed as in a dream, and I don't know how long I lay there. (*Laughs harshly*) For the first time, ever or since, I'll bet, that damned road stayed empty, and I got tired of waiting to die.

I sat up and looked off in the distance at the trees making stark silhouettes against the light of the moon and the stars twinkling hundreds of light years away, some maybe even dead but their light still streaming down. So anyhow I stood up, put on my jacket and kept on walking. (*Pause*)

So what do you think, Frank? Would I have let a car run over me if one had come along? I didn't know then, and I don't know now. But I seriously doubt I would have. I never really wanted to die . . . did I? Sometimes I had trouble knowing what was real and what was only my imagination. (*Pause*)

Pretty soon I got to Clivesville and went to see Thelma and Dick Polsky. They used to live next door. Dick was at the VFW, and Thelma wouldn't believe me when I told her what had happened. So I gulped this glass of water she handed me and stumbled outside. I'd walked eleven miles already, and it was late. I was just a kid. Seventeen years old. So I hiked back home. I told myself that if I kept up a steady pace, it wouldn't take more than a couple of hours. But that seemed like an eternity. You see, the fatigue made me colder than ever. I had no reserves to fight it. So I just kept plodding along, left foot, right foot, left foot, right foot, each step jarring my body. But I made it, Frank. The whole damn way. I stopped then and leaned against the board fence, and I was filled with hate.

I opened the gate and staggered up onto the front. The door wouldn't be locked; it never was, and I saw that someone had left the lamp on low. It was Grandma. She sat there, her face in near darkness. "Oh, Martin," she said. "I'm sorry."

There was nothing else that she could say. Really.

Questions

1. Judging from what Martin says here, what kind of life do you think he has had? Explain.

2. What kind of person is Martin? Why do you suppose he never talked about his childhood before?

3. What feelings do you think Martin has as he's talking to his friend? Do you know anyone else who has been an abused child? How do you feel about what happened to him or her?

4. Why do you suppose Martin has suddenly decided to talk about the way things used to be? What do you think his life is like now?

5. What sort of relationship do you think Martin had with his parents? His grandmother?

Playing time: Eight minutes and 40 seconds to nine minutes and 10 seconds
Character's age: 17

Soldiers' Trilogy

Ron Shaw/*Canadian*

This monologue is interspersed among other monologues that make up this performance piece illustrating how different young men react to the idea of going into military service.

The author has worked in the areas of foreign aid and development in a number of African nations, as well as in other countries.

YONKUP:

They want me for a soldier.

Big men from Mamfa have come. Their loudspeaker car, passing through the quarters, has summoned everyone to what is called a Patriots' Rally.

Mamfa is our subdivisional town and everyone who comes from Mamfa wears a uniform. Or so it seems. Policemen, health inspectors, tax collectors, the post man, they all come from Mamfa. The SDO wears a black suit with a white shirt and neck tie, but it is a uniform. He has no badges, or brass buttons, or leather belt, but it is a uniform. His is the uniform before which even soldiers and tax collectors stand with lowered eyes.

This afternoon the soldiers came as well.

They want me for a soldier and I am afraid.

Since a week now the radio has talked of the north tearing Banga in two. On market day the police inspector came with four constables and took Mallam Garba away. Mallam Garba was putting the first pieces of soja on his brazier when they seized him and beat him . . . there in front of the Banga-Bey off-license.

Everyone rushed to see.

The constables spit on Mallam Garba and chained his hands and feet. The inspector shouted that Mallam Garba was a rebel and a spy, that all Banga patriots must guard against traitors who lurk in their villages.

I am seventeen and Mallam Garba has been an old man selling spicy soja near the Banga-Bey all my life. He is blind in one eye and has often turned that eye to his brazier when I came, hungry from school, with no coins.

In the market it is said all my age mates are to become soldiers. It is said Banga needs many men. The market women, and the men in the beer halls, talk and talk. They say President Kewani is dead and a Northerner lives in government house at Yala.

It seems I have never been told the childhood village of President Kewani. Like Mallam Garba at the Banga-Bey, Massa Kewani has always been there in Yala. Still, somewhere a clan must mourn and the women go bare breasted. But in Banga, Yala and Massa Kewani have always been far away.

Today, the soldiers and their loudspeaker have brought them nearer.

In only twenty-seven days I was to take up higher studies at Mamfa. I have won my school-leaving certificate and I have passed the Holy Cross Technical College competitive examination. My mother has paid the first term fees and, with money earned selling yams from my farm, I have bought my tin box and towels and sheets and canvas shoes. How can I go for a soldier?

Injang has said she will marry me. Mama has spoken to her uncle and they are agreed.

At Holy Cross I will learn about radios and cassette players and other electrical things which go wrong. On completion of successful studies Holy Cross gives its boys a box of tools and a small loan with which to begin. In just two years I would have a shop and Injang for my wife. How can I go for a soldier?

Ambe came to my house, wearing his party sash and carrying a Banga flag. The party secretary is presenting real cloth flags to those boys who present themselves to the Major and sign their names in his book.

Tomorrow Ambe will leave Bansa and exchange his youth wing sash of red and yellow and blue for another uniform.

He was very excited, singing bits of President Kewani praise songs and laughing. Perhaps he has not heard that Massa Kewani is no longer at Yala.

Ambe says he is to be paid forty Kewans each month for soldiering, with free chop and two uniforms and new boots. The major also said, Ambe told me, that when he reaches Mera the northern girls, so tall and light, will welcome their liberators as our warrior ancestors have always been honored in victory. Why they should do that I do not understand.

Ambe is big and awkward. Injang has told me her sisters and age mates say he looks too much like his father's donkey. They think him a bit foolish. Ambe failed all four papers and was not awarded his school-leaving certificate. The gari boys in the market say his father beat him.

Ambe is happy to go for a soldier and angry that I do not wish to join him.

Ambe pressed me to go with him to the Patriots' Rally.

I did not wish to go, because I have no sash and did not want to pay money from my school fee savings to buy one. Youth wing militants selling memberships are very difficult to avoid. I also feared the Major with his book of names.

Mother said I must go, lest party militants note my absence and make trouble for our family. Also, Injang was going. She sings in her school choir and was summoned to help with the program. So I went.

I walked with Injang from her Uncle's house. She held my hand until we came to where the pressure lamps lit the street and the gathering people.

Children had brought baskets to collect the termites which fly at this season. Drawn by the many lights, insects were crashing and dying against the lamps. The street was a carpet of squirming injured termites waiting to be scooped up by laughing children.

I found a place on the step of the rice shop, across the street and far back in the crowd. I could see Ambe standing at attention in the rank of boys who had already signed the Major's book.

It must be true that President Kewani is no longer at Yala. Injang and her sisters sang the Banga national anthem and some party songs. They sang Onward Christian Soldiers and another church hymn, but there were no Massa Kewani praise songs. Everyone looked uneasy when the music ended and there had been no songs for Massa Kewani.

There was much palaver and many people shouted and clapped. The party secretary made a speech and the youth wing chairman made a longer speech.

Old Chief Acherimbe talked in Bansa but his voice was weak and he could not be heard above the cries of the children catching termites. His voice has not been heard for many years and he looked very old and very tired as two soldiers helped him stand on the beer crate and lifted him down again.

The Major from Mamfa spoke last. His words and his manner brought fear. As he talked, terror came down from the north and along the crowded street and into the hearts of the Bansa people.

When the Major spoke no one shouted or clapped. Even the children were hushed. The people listened silent and still. Though the season is now warm it seemed the damp chill of December slipped off the mountains and flowed around us.

The Major said nothing of Massa Kewani. He made his appeal to the people of Bansa in the name of the party and in the name of a General called Jata. His words called upon every strong man to join General Jata in liberating and reuniting Banga. He warned of rebels marching from the north, into the high homeland of the Bansa, burning crops and villages, violating wives and sisters, killing men and children alike, and taking slaves as was done in the days of our ancestors.

The Major said the Bansa people must sacrifice much to save life and honor in their villages. Then he announced a long list of decrees made by General Jata.

There will be new taxes in money and produce so the sons of Bansa joining the army may be fed and armed. The people must also apply to the party for ration cards to buy cooking oil, kerosine, sugar and many other things. Only those families with sons and fathers in the struggle will be issued cards. There are to be no public gatherings. Death celebrations and marriages must be postponed until Banga is whole again. Schools and colleges are closed until all of Banga is liberated.

I am to go for a soldier and I am afraid.

Questions

1. What sort of person is Yonkup? Why is he afraid? Do you think he has a right to be?

2. What is happening to Yonkup's country? How are things going to be different?

3. How do you think Yonkup feels about what is happening to his country?

4. What are the feelings Yonkup has during this monologue? Why does he have to be a soldier?

5. How do you think Yonkup's being drafted into the military is going to affect his life?

Playing time: Ten minutes and 30 seconds to eleven minutes
Character's age: 18 to 20

The Life of the Red Hat

Patrick Dieli/ *U.S.A.*

In this monologue, a gentle reminiscence, a young man is thinking back about the one time in his life he was able to make his mother happy.

The author is a playwright, a novelist, and a short story writer. To date, he has had two plays produced, one a mystery and the other about a group of people who belong to Alcoholics Anonymous.

If the monologue needs to be shorter, you can cut the first part and begin with the line, "Sister Cornilia did have a friend . . ."

PATRICK:

In her entire life, my mother claimed to have owned only two hats. The first was a small black object, the kind that fit snugly in place and came with a mesh veil attached at the front that draped over the face of the wearer. It was quite ordinary, to say the least. And Mother, never one for much make-up or jewelry, favored that hat even though it did nothing to highlight her still youthful Italian features.

And, because she wore the hat with great regularity—Sunday church services, Wednesday evening novenas and her bimonthly visits to the Immaculate Heart convent for counseling sessions, I put it in the same league with her meat loaf and mashed potatoes. Dull and duller. In fact, for some time I harbored a secret fantasy to go on a search-and-destroy mission for that hat. But, I never did. Instead I conjured up a plan to tell her how frightful she looked wearing it. Her shoulders seemed to fall forward in resignation; her physical expression lacked that certain lightness. I didn't do that either. If memory serves me well, I came down with a terminal case of cold feet.

However, inspiration came to me one day in one of the most unexpected places. Sister Cornilia Anne's eighth grade math class. If I may be allowed to digress for a moment. Sister "Slam," as she was known to more than a few students at Our Lady of Grace grammar school, besides being the guardian of my homeroom, was also the school principal. She, and she alone, according to my mother, was the proprietress of the one true foundation upon which all young Catholic boys and girls should aspire. Humble, yet forceful; caring, yet forceful; intelligent, yet forceful; we were told to study this woman, to learn from her because one day when we arrived at that critical stage of our adult lives, and had children of our own, our understanding of Sister Cornilia Anne's attributes would be there to guide us through those difficult hours. Unbeknownst to Mother, many of us had already come in direct contact with at least one of those golden attributes. And, should we be asked which one, we needed only to open a palm or bare our bottoms.

Sister Cornilia did have a friend who worked at the Valley JC Penney Department Store on the corner of Reseda Boulevard and Sherman Way. One afternoon, the time when inspiration struck, her friend appeared in the doorway of Room 103. She wasn't particularly striking, but pretty in a Donna Reed style. She wore a stylish black polka-dot dress, a pair of polished white high heels, and an unusually large red hat. That was it. The idea was planted. I knew right away I had to have that hat. If it was good enough for her, it would do just fine for mother.

When Saturday approached, I quickly collected all my savings from the several piggy banks hidden around my room. After emptying all the containers of their contents, I hastily dropped the money into my pockets and returned the empty banks to their original concealed places. Then, carefully I slipped out of the house and hurried off to Penney's. The moment was just as exciting as marching over to Billy Thompson's, the neighborhood thug, with my six brothers, prepared to meet the bully, in direct combat, to reclaim our turf. The adrenaline was flowing; I couldn't walk fast enough.

I climbed the stairs to the second floor, making a sharp right turn at the women's apparel department. It was like visiting a foreign land. Bras and girdles and slips were displayed everywhere I turned. I had seen these items in numerous department store catalogs that were mailed to our house three or four times a year. Now I was standing in the middle of the real thing. Did women really have to wear all these garments? How strange, I thought. No wonder they didn't have room for pockets.

A very official looking woman approached, smiled, and asked ever so softly if she could be of assistance. No one ever talked to me with such prettiness. It knocked the wind right out of me. Once I recovered though, I told her my purpose for being there. With that information, she knew exactly where to take me. I followed her out of the lingerie department and to the hats and coats section in the far corner of the second floor. And, it was there that I was introduced to a Miss Nancy Sherman, the woman I recognized as Sister Cornilia Anne's friend.

Of course, I didn't let on that she was the inspiration behind my mission. I could never do that. What if she told Sister and I was forced to stand up in front of the class on Monday morning and tell everyone how I spent my Saturday afternoon. God forbid such a fate would befall me! Instead, I fabricated a story about wanting to buy a hat for my mother's birthday.

She walked me through the area pointing out several different types of hats that were popular with most of her customers, unaware that the one I wanted was displayed on the metal stand behind her wooden counter. Seeing that she wasn't getting far with me, she leaned down and asked me if I had anything in particular that I wished to see. Immediately, I pointed to the object of my search. She smiled and told me I had made a very wise selection.

She pulled a large white box from a shelf beneath the counter. The box had the name JC Penney inscribed on all four sides. Slowly, she opened the case. Her eyes never left the object of my attention. Once the lid was removed, she pulled back the flimsy white tissue paper to reveal the most beautiful hat I had ever seen. It was even prettier than the one she wore, though I knew both were one and the same. I touched the brim of the hat. Petted the edges as I would the family dog, Casey. Yes, this was the hat. I nodded my approval. She produced the sales tag.

I think Miss Sherman was more than a little surprised when I emptied my pockets of all the loose bills and coins. It took her a while to sort through the lint and bubble gum wrappers. After going through everything on the counter, she told me I was short one dollar. I reached deeper into my pants pockets hoping that there was a chance I had left something inside. I squirmed as I came up empty handed.

She saw the disappointed look on my face. After a short pause, I watched as she reached into her purse and placed the additional dollar on the stack of bills and coins that rested on the counter. She smiled and said that because I looked like I really wanted the hat it would be such a disappointment if I had to leave without it. As I thanked her, she reminded me to come back at another time and return her dollar. I promised a thousand times I would. She very carefully repackaged the hat, slipped it into a large white department store shopping bag and sent me on the way. It was twenty-seven dollars well spent, I thought as I retreated down the stairs to the first floor.

On my return to our little house on Hatteras Street, I found Mother sitting in the kitchen reading the afternoon newspaper. There was very little else she liked to do in those days. I always thought that talking on the telephone and reading the paper were her favorite activities. She was a plain woman who stayed at home, fixed our meals, washed and ironed our clothes and tended to her brood of nine. She certainly wasn't given to doing much socializing. Bridge parties, parish socials, neighborhood coffee klatches; she just didn't have the time or the inclination to involve herself.

I announced I had something special for her. But first, she must close her eyes. I set the package on top of her newspaper that rested in front of her. When she reopened her eyes, she looked at me with that bewildered look of not understanding what this was all about. But, she knew me better than to ask. She simply slipped the hat box out of the bag, unfastened the wrappings, removed the lid, and when seeing what was inside, let out a small gasp. In her hands she held the red hat.

She was genuinely surprised. And, in her best motherly tone asked me where I got the money to purchase such a beautiful hat. I explained to her how I had saved my money doing odd jobs for the neighbors. She gave me a generous smile. I knew she appreciated it. She took the hat, went to the mirror in her bedroom and reappeared to thunderous applause.

For a brief moment, in our little kitchen, time seemed to change. And what a time it was. Her face was once again full of warmth. I was reminded of an earlier photograph where she stood posed alongside my father before he went off to serve with the army during the second world war.

Watching my mother surveying the hat, I couldn't help but notice how bright and lively the room now appeared. And, though the walls screamed for a fresh coat of paint, the linoleum needed repairing, and the cupboards were missing knobs and screws, the wide-brimmed red hat was all that counted.

Tears filled her eyes. The soiled dress she wore was now spotless and freshly pressed. Her disheveled, thick, black hair shone beneath her newly found crown. She pulled me into her arms and thanked me for the gift. The magic of the red hat filled the house.

And then my father entered the room. He saw the hat and said nothing. I knew he wasn't the sentimental type; I avoided any such displays whenever he was around. But, this time it was different. The light hitting the hat caught him off balance. He seemed eager to walk into it. He wanted to say something but couldn't. He let his eyes speak for him. They looked lovingly at her.

Mother stood there embarrassed. She wasn't used to this sort of attention. Time hadn't been kind to her. The hardship of the years had taken their toll. Nervously, she reached to pull the hat off. But father raised a hand in protest. He approached her. Tenderly, he took his hands and caressed her face. This was so strange coming from him. He reached down for her hand as he placed an arm around her waist and started to dance. Together, they waltzed around the room. I sat at the table, smiled, and watched as they covered the entire kitchen never once speaking or recognizing that there wasn't a sound of music to be heard. But, dance they did.

When they stopped, mother covered her face to hide her tears. She excused herself, quickly leaving the room. My father followed after her. I heard the door to their room close.

I remained in the kitchen a while longer watching two silhouettes gliding about the floor. I looked at the empty box, smiled, and then went outside and sat on the front porch with old Casey.

Several years later, when my mother died, I was rummaging through a few of her old possessions when I came across the container with the red hat. I opened it and found a small card pinned to its rim. The note was handwritten by my mother. It read—"This was a gift. It was a wonderful red hat."

Questions

1. Why is the hat now so important to the young man who is delivering the monologue?

2. Why do you think the young man bought his mother the hat? What surprises were there as a result of this?

3. How did the boy feel about his mother when he bought her the hat? How does he feel now?

4. What do you think should be the prevailing mood of this piece? Explain.

5. Do you like the monologue? Why?

Playing time: Four minutes and 45 seconds to
five minutes and 15 seconds
Character's age: 12

Hate Child

Art Specht/ *U.S.A.*

This monologue is taken from a longer piece that deals
with the supernatural, with a "hate child" who wants the boy
to come to her and make her real. He resists her as long as he
can, and then is forced to go to the island where she is waiting
for him.

The author has written many short stories and several
novels, often from the viewpoint of a twelve-year-old boy.

CHARLIE BOB:

It was Sunday, the morning of my twelfth birthday. My daddy was passed out in his hammock on the porch, his mouth hanging open, a half-drank jar of shine underneath his hammock. A flock of flies had come through the punched out window screens and was buzzing around his head, while the tip of his tongue poked out over his bottom lip like the end of an old yellow sponge. He'd clean forgot it was my birthday, never even bought me a present like he used to do before my mama left us.

I was feeling awful sorry for myself, setting in that old wicker chair watching him. I recollected when my mama was alive on my eleventh birthday, the big chocolate cake she'd made, how all them kids had come over and stuffed themselves with ice cream and cake and played pin-the-tail-on-the-donkey. I got all watery eyed. My mama died in a car accident one month later.

I was thinking hard about her when all of sudden I heard this voice whispering inside my head. The hair on my neck prickled and goose bumps jumped up all over me. I thought for a second it was my mama talking to me from the grave. Then the voice came again, and I knew it wasn't her. It was a young gal's voice that I'd never heard before.

"Charlie Bob," she called, like she was a long distance away. "Come see me. I'm at the old Bodine house. Got a chocolate cake that I made special for your birthday."

It scared me, hearing someone talk inside my head that way, because I figured I might be getting one of them mental breakdowns. Lately, I'd been under a heap of strain doing all them chores for the rent money. I knew if we got thrown out on the streets, them social workers would put me in an orphanage. My daddy had promised me he'd quit drinking and get a job, only he never done it. He'd stuck his nose in the bottle after my mama died and couldn't get it out.

"Charlie Bob, did you hear me?" she called again, only a heap louder this time.

Popping straight up in my chair, I waved the flies away from my face and looked around, seeing if one of my friends had snuck up on me. Jimmy Lee's sister had sent away for one of them gadgets you stick in your mouth to throw your voice with, and I figured she might be around. She loved to play practical jokes, only it wasn't her. There wasn't nobody on the porch, except me and my daddy.

Lord, I'm sure enough hearing things, I thought. I eyed that jar of shine under my daddy's hammock. I'd sneaked a nip of that stuff a couple times just to see how come my daddy drank it so much, but I never liked the taste. It burnt my mouth and made tears come to my eyes. Now I figured maybe I ought to take a swig to clear my head of that gal's voice. I even reckoned I might be coming down with the flu bug and was getting crazy with fever. I felt my forehead, but it was real cool.

"I'm waiting on you, Charlie Bob," she said, clear as spring water. Her voice was sweet and ripply like a stream running downhill. "Got a nice chocolate cake and presents for you. It'll be a party just like your mama used to have."

This time I jumped clean out of my chair. "Hush up!" I yelled at my head. "You're gonna get us both put in the bughouse."

It didn't do a nickel's worth of good, yelling at my head that way. She kept on calling me until her voice wasn't sweet no more—got peskier than yellow jackets whining in my ears. "Hurry up, Charlie Bob, I'm waiting on you," she sang over and over again until I figured I'd go nuts.

"Okay, okay," I hollered, when I finally couldn't stand it no more. "Hush up, whoever you are. If you'll quit nagging at me, I just might go out to that old Bodine house."

Right away, she quit yammering and was quiet. I'd just told her I might go out there to hush her up. I wouldn't go out to the old Bodine place if she jumped out of my head and handed me a hundred dollar bill. That old house was on the other side of town way back in them swamps. I'd heard old timers say that after the War Between the States, the river flooded a bunch of plantations and left a couple underwater. The Bodine house was one of them. It set on a small chunk of land with big cypress and swamp all around it. Most of the roof had fallen in and nobody had lived there for fifty years. Way back before I was born, some rich feller bought it. He tried to make it over like new, but some of his workers got sucked down in quicksand and the others caught fever. He gave up on the place and willed it to his heirs. They let the house set there all this time, mainly on account of nobody would buy it.

Another reason you couldn't drag me to that old place with a swamp buggy is because everybody in Atkinville claimed it was haunted. Folks stayed away from there, even the fellers who made their living trapping and poaching gators in the swamps. I wasn't about to go out to that creepy old house, but I figured I had to tell her something to keep her from driving me buggy.

Slipping out the screen door, I headed for the middle of town acting like I was still thinking about going out to that Bodine place so's to fool her.

Questions

1. What sort of person is Charlie Bob? If you met him, do you think you'd like him? Why?

2. What is Charlie Bob's life like?

3. Why do you think the "voice" chooses his head to be in?

4. How does Charlie Bob feel about his father? About his life in general?

5. What do you think will happen if Charlie Bob goes over to the Bodine house?

Playing time: Nine to ten minutes
Character's age: 19 or 20

Delusions

Zachary Thomas/ *U.S.A.*

Delusions is a play about a young man who fled from a
Catholic seminary where he had gone to study for the
priesthood. He left Pittsburgh after discovering his parish
priest was not the idol he'd thought him to be. Using all the
money he had, he bought a Greyhound bus ticket. He wanted
to get as far away as his money would take him.

He ends up in a little coal mining town and soon joins the
Army Air Corps. Somewhat mentally unbalanced to begin
with, he becomes worse and worse, seeking to find Yahweh's
plan for his life. Finally, after being shot down in Japan, he
crosses over completely into insanity when he jumps up on a
barrel in the prisoner of war camp screaming that not only can
he reveal all the military secrets of both the U.S. and
Germany, but he can reveal God's plan for all of humanity.

Six months later, he's sent to Fort Sam Houston where
he's placed in the psycho ward. In this scene, he seems fairly
rational while talking to his psychiatrist. But this is an act to
make the doctor think he's recovering his sanity.

JOHN:

Most days it was hot enough to feel the heat right through the soles of my black regulation shoes. But I didn't care. I'd been accepted for cadet training, and that's all that mattered. I'd passed the tests and was going to fly. Me, John O'Shaughnessy, who'd never even been close to a plane until the last couple of months.

I hadn't been up yet. That would come later. But I'd taken my basic training at Buckley Field, just outside Denver. I loved it. Not everything I had to put up with—half of it KP, up at 0230, scrubbing pots and pans—but just being alive on God's earth. A different part of the earth than I'd ever expected to see.

Mountainous, like Somerset County, Pennsylvania, to which I'd escaped from Pittsburgh. But the rock-studded mountains were so high I had to throw back my head to see to the snow-covered tops. And air not choked with fumes from steel mill stacks or burning slag heaps, but clear and pure.

I loved Colorado and was sorry to leave. Yet the only thing that mattered was that I'd passed all the tests, physical and mental. Passed with flying colors. So I was sent to Minter Field, a pre-cadet, waiting for an opening to begin my pilot's training.

I didn't understand why I wanted that so badly. But I did, even though up to then I'd been earthbound, my only acquaintance with planes that of observer as they flew high above the Mount Troy section of Pittsburgh where I'd lived.

I thought of one of the promises my father had made and broken: to give me a ride in a plane for my birthday. But every birthday came and went, and there was never a ride.

Well, I was going to show him; I'd not only ride in planes, I'd fly them.

Other than daily drills, PT and KP, there was little to do. I didn't mind the discipline there or at Buckley Field as much as most of the other guys. Coming from seminary, I was used to it, I guess, used to an ordered life, to strictness, to blindly obeying rules.

One morning after I dressed, I looked outside. It was 0600 and already hot. Minter Field was part of a giant bowl where heat and air pollution seemed to lie like smoke in a bottle. Yet it was beautiful country too, with groves of orange and lemon trees and vast fields of potatoes.

And any day now there were bound to be some openings. That's why I felt like whistling or praising God or both on my way to morning formation. Instead, the noncom officer led the guys in a stupid song, that didn't make any sense. "I used to work in Chicago; I used to work in Chicago." I didn't say anything. I had trouble making friends, maybe because of my seminary training, I don't know. So I kept up the pretense of happy-go-lucky, would-be flyboy.

We stopped outside the mess hall for "an important announcement." Major Reynolds stood before us, a fat little man with red hair and freckles. He looked from face to face, and then glanced down at a sheet of paper he held, then up again. I wondered what was going on.

Let me tell you, when I found out, I felt my knees sag and my face grow hot and my throat become thick. I thought it was a joke, some kind of sick joke. There wouldn't be any pilot training. Not for me nor the others. We were washed out. "At the convenience of the government." Some stupid so-and-so decided we were needed elsewhere. So to hell with our tests, our records, our hopes.

When Reynolds finished, it was quiet, absolute silence. Then they started to sing. " Off we go into the wild blue yonder, flying high." Well, I didn't want any part in that. No, sir.

We came to a group of cadets, real ones, men who *would* go on to be pilots. They were hanging out their barracks' windows. "Boo hoo! Can't be a pilot," they yelled. "Go home to mama! Boo hoo!" I wanted to kill them. Guess I shouldn't say that, should I, doc?

But if I ever caught one of them alone, I thought to myself, I'd beat him to a pulp. The hell with the pretense of holding your head up high. The hell with the damned Army and the Air Corps and the idiots who decided to wash us out.

So then I went to Kingman, Arizona, the worst place I'd ever been. Nothing but sand and cactus. Cacti. One of the men said it could be beautiful in the spring, filled with all these exotic flowers. I didn't believe it. I hated the heat which tricked you into believing it wasn't hot because there was no humidity. Heat that hit my body like a blast from a steel mill furnace, that gave me a constant body rash that the base doctor said could only be helped by lying naked with a fan blowing. Where in the hell would I get a fan or have the time and privacy to use it?

Up until now I'd liked the Army, tolerated the stupid parts because I knew it would be worth it. Oh, sure, Doc, I was still going to fly. In the ball turret. Hell, before this I hadn't even known what a ball turret was. Now I knew all right. The most vulnerable part of a B-17. (*He laughs.*)

I learned that by pushing and pulling on the two handles you could turn the turret whatever way you wanted, up, down, around. I learned to push the buttons that fired the guns.

I felt frightened and small compared to all below me. What did my heavenly father want from me? I wondered. I'd tried to do my best. Now Papa Yahweh didn't want me to be a priest or a pilot. Surely, it wasn't that he wanted me to be a ball turret gunner. And when the war was over, would I spend my life in a Royal Bituminous Coal Company mine, lungs filling with black dust, joints getting stiff with the dampness?

Yet I had to trust Papa and Lord Baby. They knew best. They had a plan for my life. I hated what I was doing. I was one of the tallest men to be chosen for my job, a job for a little man. I'm five-eight and could barely curl up to fit in the damned ball turret.

Sometimes the stupid pilots flew through the Grand Canyon, a few hundred feet off the ground. Air currents bumped us up and down, making me dizzy and sick. So I learned to stare at spots on the distant horizon to keep from throwing up. I guess the pilots thought it was funny. (*His voice becomes harsh.*)

My arms and legs went to sleep; I couldn't stretch. I cramped and could barely stand the pain. There was nothing to eat; there wasn't room. Most of the time I spent on my back, like lying inside a giant clam shell.

Well, let me tell you, I learned to fire, or pretend fire, at planes that flashed across the screen and to identify Zeros or German FockeWulfs or Heinkels or Messerchmitts. And I was the best they had. A mere fraction of a second was all it took for me to identify what flashed and was gone. And you know, Doc, sometimes I wished maybe I wouldn't be so fast. I wished maybe I'd wash out of gunnery school as well.

But something inside drove me to excel. Maybe it was that Papa Yahweh did have a plan after all.

So in the simulated firings I hit the Zeros and the Heinkels more often than not. I hit the ground targets, and in the evenings I was free to do what I wanted—to go for ice cream, to read my Bible I always kept within reach, to be thankful to Yahweh in heaven that I was alive and well, even though I had to be a damn ball turret gunner instead of a pilot.

Well, Doc, at the end of three months I was ordered to Lincoln, Nebraska, to be assigned to a crew, and then to Dyersburg, Tennessee, my last stop before being sent overseas.

(*Pause*) And it was worse than I expected. My eleventh mission, March 3, 1943. I'll always remember that date, burned deep into the middle of my brain.

It was early morning, outside Tokyo. Suddenly, a Zero appeared out of nowhere, spitting fire. I rotated the turret, fired back, missed and felt like I'd been in a train going full speed slamming into a wall. (*With increasing agitation*) We went into a nose-dive, righted ourselves, then plunged straight down. I rotated the turret and fumbled at the hatch. I had no parachute; there wasn't enough room. I had to get inside the plane, praying to Yahweh I'd make it. God wouldn't let me end up with my body smashed and broken on an island off Asia. God wouldn't do it, Lord Baby be praised.

Well, sir, I pushed and clawed through the hatch, reached for a parachute. The plane gave a lurch. I saw men jumping. I strapped on the chute, checked to make sure it was okay and crawled out into space.

I felt bile rise in my throat. But I counted off and pulled the ring. I felt a jolt, gravity pulling me one way, the parachute another. I looked up to see a billowing cloud directly above my head and felt a tremendous sense of relief.

Questions

1. Why do you think John didn't mind military life as much as the other men with him?

2. Why was being a pilot so important to John?

3. What touches of John's insanity can you see in this monologue? Explain.

4. Why do you suppose John refers to God as Yahweh and Jesus as Lord Baby?

5. What could be John's reasons for trying to appear more sane than he is in this monologue?

Playing time: Four minutes and 15 seconds to
four minutes and 45 seconds
Character's age: Probably about 18

The House of Blue Leaves

John Guare/*U.S.A.*

The action of this play occurs in 1965, when Pope Paul is
coming to New York to say mass at Yankee Stadium. Artie
Shaughnessy, a zookeeper, dreams while asleep that his son
Ronnie is pope. While awake, he dreams of becoming a
songwriter. An example of his lyrics is, "Where's the devil in
Evelyn?"

In this monologue Ronnie Shaughnessy has gone AWOL
from Army basic training to come home and blow up the
pope. As he speaks, he is wiring a homemade bomb.

RONNIE:

My father tell you all about me? Pope Ronnie? Charmed life? How great I am? That's how he is with you. You should hear him with me, you'd sing a different tune pretty quick, and it wouldn't be "Where Is the Devil in Evelyn?" (*He exits into his room and comes out a moment later, carrying a large, dusty box. He opens it. From it, he takes a bright red altar boy cassock and surplice that fit him when he was twelve. He speaks to us as he dresses.*) I was twelve years old and all the newspapers had headlines on my twelfth birthday that Billy was coming to town. And *Life* was doing stories on him and *Look* and the newsreels because Billy was searching America to find the Ideal American Boy to play Huckleberry Finn. And Billy came to New York and called my father and asked him if he could stay here—Billy needed a hideout. In Waldorf Astorias all over the country, chambermaids would wheel silver carts to change the sheets. And out of the sheets would hop little boys saying, "Hello, I'm Huckleberry Finn." All over the country, little boys dressed in blue jeans and straw hats would be sent to him in crates, be under the silver cover covering his dinner, his medicine cabinet in all his hotel rooms, his suitcase— "Hello, hello, I'm Huckleberry Finn." And he was coming here to hide out. Here—Billy coming here—I asked the nun in school who was Huckleberry Finn—

The nun in Queen of Martyrs knew. She told me. The Ideal American Boy. And coming home, all the store windows reflected me and the mirror in the tailor shop said, "Hello, Huck." The butcher shop window said, "Hello, Huck. Hello, Huckleberry Finn. All America wants to meet Billy and he'll be hiding out in your house." I came home—went in there—into my room and packed my bag. . . . I knew Billy would see me and take me back to California with him that very day. This room smelled of ammonia and air freshener and these slipcovers were new that day and my parents were filling up the icebox in their brand-new clothes, filling up the icebox with food and liquor as excited as if the Pope was coming—and nervous because they hadn't seen him in a long while—Billy. They told me my new clothes were on my bed. To go get dressed. I didn't want to tell them I'd be leaving shortly to start a new life. That I'd be flying out to California with Billy on the H.M.S. *Huckleberry*. I didn't want tears from them—only trails of envy. . . . I went to my room and packed my bag and waited.

The doorbell rang. (*Starts hitting two notes on the piano.*) If you listen close, you can still hear the echoes of those wet kisses and handshakes and tears and backs getting hit and "Hello, Billy's, Hello." They talked for a long time about people from their past. And then my father called out: "Ronnie, guess who? Billy, we named him after your father. Ronnie, guess who?"

I picked up my bag and said goodbye to myself in the mirror. Came out. Billy there. Smiling.

It suddenly dawned on me. You had to do things to get parts.

I began dancing. And singing. Immediately. Things I have never done in my life—before or since. I stood on my head and skipped and whirled—(*He does a cartwheel.*) spectacular leaps in the air so I could see veins in the ceiling—ran up and down the keys of the piano and sang and began laughing and crying soft and loud to show off all my emotions. And I heard music and drums that I couldn't even keep up with. And then cut off all my emotions just like that. Instantly. And took a deep bow like the Dying Swan I saw on Ed Sullivan. I picked up my suitcase and waited by the door.

Billy turned to my parents, whose jaws were down to about there, and Billy said, "You never told me you had a mentally retarded child. You never told me I had an idiot for a godchild," and I picked up my bag and went into my room and shut the door and never came out the whole time he was here.

My only triumph was he could never find a Huckleberry Finn. Another company made the picture a few years later, but it flopped.

My father thinks I'm nothing. Billy. My sergeant. They laugh at me. You laughing at me? I'm going to fool you all. By tonight, I'll be on headlines all over the world. Cover of *Time. Life.* TV specials. (*Shows a picture of himself on the wall.*) I hope they use this picture of me—I look better with hair—go ahead—laugh. Because you know what I think of you? (*Gives us hesitant Bronx cheers.*) I'm sorry you had to hear that—pay seven or eight dollars to hear that. But I don't care. I'll show you all. I'll be too big for any of you.

Questions

1. What type of person do you think Ronnie is? Why?

2. Why do you suppose he wants to blow up the pope?

3. Why do you think Ronnie wanted so desperately to be picked to play Huckleberry Finn?

4. Is this monologue realistic? Is it believable? Explain.

5. Ronnie obviously is doing something that is not normal—wiring a bomb to blow up the pope. How would you go about presenting him to an audience?

Playing time: Four minutes to four minutes and 30 seconds

Character's age: Late teens

Curse of the Starving Class

Sam Shepard/*U.S.A.*

Curse of the Starving Class takes place in a farmhouse kitchen in California. Wesley and Emma are the son and daughter of Weston and Ella. The family is near the end, both financially and emotionally.

As the action in this monologue begins, Wesley is picking up the debris left when his father broke down the door the previous night.

WESLEY:

(*As he throws wood into wheelbarrow.*) I was lying there on my back. I
could smell the avocado blossoms. I could hear the coyotes. I could
hear stock cars squealing down the street. I feel myself in my bed in
my room in this house in this town in this state in this country. I
could feel this country close like it was part of my bones. I could feel
the presence of all the people outside, at night, in the dark. Even
sleeping people I could feel. Even all the sleeping animals. Dogs.
Peacocks. Bulls. Even tractors sitting in the wetness, waiting for the
sun to come up. I was looking straight up at the ceiling at all my
model airplanes hanging by all their thin metal wires. Floating.
Swaying very quietly like they were being blown by someone's
breath. Cobwebs moving with them. Dust laying on their wings.
Decals peeling off their wings. My P-39. My Messerchmitt. My Jap
Zero. I could feel myself lying far below them on my bed like I was
on the ocean and overhead they were on reconnaissance. Scouting
me. Floating. Taking pictures of the enemy. Me, the enemy. I could
feel the space around me like a big, black world. I listened like an
animal. My listening was afraid. Afraid of sound. Tense. Like any
second something could invade me. Some foreigner. Something
indescribable. Then I heard the Packard coming up the hill. From a
mile off I could tell it was the Packard by the sound of the valves.
The lifters have a sound like nothing else. Then I could picture my
dad driving it. Shifting unconsciously. Downshifting into second for
the last pull up the hill. I could feel the headlights closing in. Cut-
ting through the orchard. I could see the trees being lit one after the
other by the lights, then going back to black. My heart was pounding. Just from my Dad coming back. Then I heard him pull the
brake. Lights go off. Key's turned off. Then a long silence. Him just
sitting in the car. Just sitting. I picture him just sitting. What's he
doing? Just sitting. Waiting to get out. Why's he waiting to get out?
He's plastered and can't move. He's plastered and doesn't want to
move. He's going to sleep there all night. He's slept there before.
He's woken up with dew on the hood before. Freezing headache.
Teeth covered with peanuts. Then I hear the door of the Packard
open. A pop of metal. Dogs barking down the road. Door slams.
Feet. Paper bag being tucked under one arm. Paper bag covering
"Tiger Rose." Feet coming. Feet walking toward the door. Feet
stopping. Heart pounding. Sound of door not opening. Foot kicking
door. Man's voice. Dad's voice. Dad calling Mom. No answer. Foot
kicking. Foot kicking harder. Wood splitting. Man's voice. In the
night. Foot kicking hard through door. One foot right through

door. Bottle crashing. Glass breaking. Fist through door. Man cursing. Man going insane. Feet and hands tearing. Head smashing. Man yelling. Shoulder smashing. Whole body crashing. Woman screaming. Mom screaming. Mom screaming for police. Man throwing wood. Man throwing up. Mom calling cops. Dad crashing away. Back down driveway. Car door slamming. Ignition grinding. Wheels screaming. First gear grinding. Wheels screaming off down hill. Packard disappearing. Sound disappearing. No sound. No sight. Planes still hanging. Heart still pounding. No sound. Mom crying soft. Soft crying. Then no sound. Then softly crying. Then moving around through house. Then no moving. Then crying softly. Then stopping. Then, far off the freeway could be heard.

Questions

1. What do you think Wesley is feeling as he's picking up the debris from the door's being smashed in? How would you try to show this for an audience?

2. Why do you suppose Wesley speaks in such choppy sentences toward the end? Why does he repeat so much?

3. Why do you think Wesley says his model airplanes were scouting the enemy which was himself? What did he mean by this?

4. Do you think you would like Wesley as a person? Explain.

5. Do you like this monologue? Why? If you had a choice, would you like to present it to an audience?

Playing time: Two minutes and 50 seconds to
three minutes and 10 seconds
Character's age: 17 or 18

Brontosaurus

Lanford Wilson/ *U.S.A.*

A rich, lonely woman of forty-five is an antique dealer.
She has invited her nephew, who will be attending college,
to share her New York apartment.

She is very talkative; he is a blunt theology student of few
words. They have nothing in common, yet, even though she
complains constantly about the nephew, she wants desperately to gain his affection.

The nephew finally announces that he is moving out. The
antique dealer then makes remarks about his "calling" to the
ministry, telling him to imagine a bricklayer or fireman being
"called" to his occupation.

In this monologue, the nephew speaks out for the first
time in more than monosyllables to relate his story.

NEPHEW:

(*Straightforward*) I was standing at the side of the house. I don't remember what I had been doing. I don't remember anything before, immediately before, or immediately after. I stood for a while and then I went inside. I was standing at the side of the house. I had come from around behind in the shade and was standing in the sun; not doing anything, not going anywhere, just standing at the side of the house in the sun. And the hand of God reached out and touched me. That doesn't mean anything. It's abstract, isn't it? But it's the easiest way of explaining the feeling. (*Dealer sits*) I was standing there, not thinking anything that I would remember. There was a bush on my left and the corner of the house on my right. Instead of just stopping for a while and then moving on, while I was stopped I became aware that my body was changing, or something was happening, physically happening, inside my body. As if all my cells were changing at the same time. Some vibrating sensation through my body that raised me or made me feel like I was physically growing, like a—perhaps a chemical change was occurring. And I started to get scared, but instead of that happening it was gradually like I wasn't standing there anymore. For a moment it was like I had changed into a gas. I felt I was spreading, thinning out, being led over the world or shown the world. Thinning out to take it all in, to absorb it. Or I was shown what I was. I heard people speaking in languages that I understood but had never heard before, I heard bells—no, I didn't actually *hear* anything, but I seemed to *know* about bells in church towns, in the farm country around small towns where they make wine, in France; and people getting up where it was just beginning to be light, to go to work; people walking on streets, shopping, and small things growing in the wet and shade in rain forests. I didn't see them, I wasn't shown them, I just knew them. Because thinning out, or whatever it was, I *became* them. An old lady who thought in a language different from the one she spoke, dying in terrible pain in the geriatric ward of a very efficient hospital; twins just being born in the Orient; a boy my age, in India, whose job was to carry the censer with incense, swinging it, in a Catholic church: I didn't know them, I *was* them. I was *they*. They were me. We were all the same stuff, the same regenerating impulse. I just thinned out to mix with it all or to realize what I was, what I had come from, and gradually came back to my own design, my own body. But, of course, I thought about it differently, because it wasn't mine. I wasn't me. I was them. I was they.

Questions

1. What do you think about the things the nephew described as happening to him? Do you think they did or could happen? Why?

2. Why do you think the nephew felt he was experiencing all these things? How do you suppose this changed his life?

3. Describe the nephew's beliefs and convictions. What can you tell about the type of person he is from what he says?

4. Why do you suppose the nephew has finally decided to talk, to tell his aunt of his experience?

5. Why do you think the nephew and the antique dealer have continued to live together when they are such opposites?

Playing time: Seven minutes to seven minutes
and 30 seconds
Character's age: 18 or 19

Night Walk

Carl Catt/*U.S.A.*

Night Walk is part of a longer autobiographical piece about
a summer the author spent working at a national park. The
monologue is self-contained, telling everything you need to
know to follow it from when the narrator gets off the bus to
his fear of the rattlesnakes.

Catt is a retired university professor and also has taught
non-college classes in writing. Short stories he's written have
appeared in a number of literary journals.

CARL:

The Greyhound bus driver said he wasn't supposed to stop between towns. I made up a *granny's dying* story. He grinned, slowed to a stop and let me off at the remote wooded cross roads. I left the highway and walked up the narrow road leading into the woods. The trees were huge. Their branches interlaced overhead. It was like a cool tunnel, a refuge.

I was returning to my lifeguard job at Beaver Lake State Park after a weekend with forestry school buddies.

Ahead of me lay ten miles of narrow blacktop meandering through the woods, dead-ending at the park. I tossed my small canvas bag into the air and ran, fantasizing football as I caught it cradled in my arms. There were lots of cars coming out of the park, but none were going in. It was late afternoon. "Stupid ass," I said, "I'll never catch a ride this time of day."

It was getting darker and there was no moon. The tree crowns over the road left a scattering of small dead branches. Even though the air was cool, I heard crickets. Soon there were thousands of them screeching like demons in the night. It kinda scared me. I loved it.

I recalled a trip on the road weeks ago with Ralph and Leon, two campers from a small college in Maryland. One night we drove to town to see a double feature. It was after midnight when we left the highway and started up the narrow blacktop to the park.

I was flabbergasted by all the snakes on the road. A few had been hit by cars and thrashed about on the pavement. Some of the undamaged snakes stared into the headlights. They were blinded, I supposed, because they too slithered about aimlessly. Ralph swerved side to side, running over the snakes. Two or three times we stopped to look. Some could still raise their heads a few inches and strike at us, but they couldn't wriggle off the road. The sound of their quivering rattles riveted me with fear. That night Ralph killed over twenty snakes, eleven of which were rattlers.

Ralph said that on cool nights, snakes, being cold-blooded animals, like to move onto roads because the blacktop stays warm long after sundown.

My thoughts of snakes and friends faded as I saw the flat spreading branches of an old white pine up ahead. In the near darkness, it was like a huge layered sculpture. To my side was a hemlock with its drooping twigs silhouetted against the sky. In spite of the darkness, it wasn't difficult to follow the road. There were openings between many of the trees, making a path of lighter darkness. I was laughing to myself about *lighter darkness* when I stepped on a stick. If I tripped and hurt myself, I'd be all alone five or six miles now from either the park or the highway. I hadn't seen a car for more than an hour.

The ride up the road with Ralph and Leon that evening flashed across my mind again when I stepped on another stick. Suppose it had been . . . a flash of fear engulfed me. I was suddenly sweaty, cold, shaking. I stopped, couldn't move. The next step might be on a rattlesnake. Soft, giving somewhat, rolling under my foot like a rope—a thick rope wrapped in soft cloth. But it wouldn't be a rope. It would be alive. I'd be able to feel its muscles move through the soft sole of my worn out sneakers. Its muscles would tense up instantly. I wouldn't have time to remove my foot, no matter how quick I was. There I would be with my foot on a snake. The thing would twist around. I would be helpless, standing stiff and frightened. The feel of something hitting my pants leg and the sharp prick of its fangs—it would be like an electric shock.

I didn't have a snake bite kit, but I did have my pen knife. But it was dark. I couldn't see the fang marks. I wouldn't know where to make the X-cuts on my leg to bleed out the poison. Keep calm, I cautioned myself, it was only a stick I stepped on. A stick is hard. It wouldn't move except to roll under my foot. On a country road like this there are lots of sticks. I wondered if every stick I stepped on would feel like a snake. The crickets screamed louder. I was scared. I vowed to wait all night at that very spot. If I didn't walk, didn't take a step, I couldn't step on a rattlesnake.

Finally, I walked on. With each step I grew more accustomed to the fear. After a while, I walked much easier. I didn't step on any sticks. I calmed down. I had been ridiculous. After all, there were only about twenty snakes that night with Ralph and Leon. Only about half were rattlers.

It was so dark now that I couldn't see the silhouettes of the hills, but I was sure that the park was close by. I walked faster, knowing that my ordeal was almost over. I breathed easy, swung my arms and laughed. Then I stepped on something soft. It rolled under my foot like rope wrapped in cloth. Something thumped against my Levis. I felt a pin prick pain on my left leg. I dropped my canvas bag and ran up the road. My lungs burned with pain, but I kept running, sucking in air and blowing it out again. I stopped, rubbed the sweat out of my eyes, saw the lights of the park ranger's cabin. I ran to it, falling against the door, pounding on it until my hands hurt. Then I screamed for help. Nobody answered.

I stumbled to my cabin and fumbled for the key over the door. It dropped. I frantically scrambled on my hands and knees, patting the soil searching for the key. Then I stood up quickly. I trembled. Snakes might be there, ready to bite me in the face. I moved my feet slowly, feeling for the key. At last I felt it, bent my knees, lowered myself to within arm's reach of the ground and snatched it up. I felt the door, found the lock. The key slipped away from the hole when I tried to push it up. "Go in," I pleaded. Finally, it slipped into place, I opened the door, switched on the light, searched my leg for the fang marks. I couldn't find them. The sharp, burning pain of the snake's bite that I'd felt only minutes ago was gone. I sat on my bed and whispered, "Fool, I stepped on a stick, that's all, just a stick."

After I rested, I took my flashlight off the bookcase and walked back to the road to get my bag. I walked slowly, searching the path ahead of me with the light. The bag lay on its side in the middle of the road. I picked it up. Through the chorus of night sounds, I heard a faint rattling. I swept the area around me with the light. Halfway across the road I saw a rattlesnake. It was a yard or more long and fat as my arm. It was crushed and almost immobile and covered with blood. I moved closer and pointed my light at the snake. It's head was misshaped. Its huge mouth opened like a yawn and then closed.

I ran back to the cabin, scanning the path ahead of me with the light. I sat on my bunk, took off my right sneaker, then the left one. There was blood imbedded in its tread.

Questions

1. Do you think the narrator's fear of being bitten by a rattlesnake was logical? Explain. How would you react in a similar situation?

2. In what way did the narrator let his imagination make him more afraid?

3. What is the prevailing mood of this piece? Explain.

4. What could the narrator have done to avoid feeling terrified?

5. Where did the blood on the tread of the shoe come from?

Playing time: Two minutes and 45 seconds to
three minutes and 5 seconds
Character's age: 13

Because of Romek

James D. Kitchen and David Faber/*U.S.A.*

It is several decades after World War II, and David Faber,
who survived internment in many concentration camps, is
asked to identify the man who tortured and killed his brother
during the war. Romek Faber was working for the under-
ground resistance movement, seeking to prevent Germany
from developing the atomic bomb.

In the dramatic account of a true story entitled *Because of
Romek,* the visit with these German investigators makes
David remember once more everything that happened to
him as a teenaged Jewish boy in Poland at the start of World
War II.

In this scene, Romek has fixed a hiding place for the family,
except there isn't time for David's father to reach this place,
so he is the first of his family to die. One by one all the others
are killed by the Nazis, except David, who made a promise to
his mother that he'd stay alive and tell everything that
happened.

DAVID:

One night, all of us were sitting around the table Romek and I had carried home from an empty apartment downstairs. Suddenly we heard footsteps on the stairs which came three flights straight up from the street.

"It's the Germans!" Romek said. "Quick! Hide!"

Sonia was the first to step on the chair, climb onto the wardrobe and scramble through the hole. The other girls were right behind, then Mother and I. Romek hurried in after us and pulled the picture into place.

We heard a crash, then the sound of footsteps and a rough voice.

"Nobody here!"

"They're hiding! Look, the window's open." This one sounded younger.

"Under the roof like the ones we found yesterday."

We held our breath and listened to them climb out the window. Their boots scraped on the tiles.

Mother gripped Romek's arm.

"Where's Papa!" she whispered. "Why didn't he hide with us!"

Romek groaned. "There wasn't time, Mama," he said. "He hid under the roof."

"Oh, my God! They'll kill him!" Mother's voice shook. We heard tiles breaking and sliding.

"Here's one!"

More words we couldn't understand. The thud of blows. A scream.

We heard the Germans jump down from the window as they came back into the room.

"We got one, anyhow." It was the younger voice.

"Ja! Hiding like a rat!" the rough voice laughed. "Come on."

In the darkness behind the wall, I reached for Mother. We clung to each other, crying without a sound.

The soldiers tramped across the floor and down the stairs.

"Go look for Papa, Romek," Mother whispered.

"We'd better wait a few minutes to be sure they've gone."

We heard a thump, then slow footsteps. Someone was in the room. Maybe it's a trick, I thought. Maybe one of the soldiers stayed behind. But why would he make noise?

A creak. Someone opened the wardrobe door. Slow steps again. Quiet.

We waited for what seemed like hours, afraid to talk or move.

Finally, Romek whispered, "I think they're gone. We've got to see about Papa."

I slipped past him, out onto the wardrobe. In the candlelight, I saw a white form on Father's straw sack. Without saying anything, I jumped down to the floor. Blood lay on the bare boards in a path from the window to the wardrobe. I followed it to the sack.

Father lay there. Blood oozed from cuts on his head, staining his tallis. More blood showed through the white cloth he had put on, like a kittel. His hands were folded across his chest.

I stared, frozen, for a moment. Then I cried out, "Romek! Mama!"

They came quickly. Mother knelt by the bed, crying in great sobs. She picked up Father's hands, and held them against her lips.

The Germans had beaten Father and cut him with axes, but somehow he had managed to get inside, get his prayer shawl and the white garment from the wardrobe, put them on and lie down.

Romek lifted Mother to her feet.

"Mama, Mama," he said softly. He held her, and when her sobs stopped, he murmured, "He died with dignity, Mama. Not in the street."

Questions

1. Why do you think it was so important to David Faber to tell his story about World War II?

2. This period in history is now called the Holocaust, which means extermination or slaughter. How do you think something like this was allowed to happen?

3. Put yourself in David's place. How would you react? What feelings is David experiencing as he tells about what happened?

4. How could you communicate the horror and brutality of this scene to an audience?

5. At first David Faber had refused to meet with the Germans who were investigating war crimes. Why do you suppose this is so?

Performance Information Chart

CLASSICAL THEATRE

Monologues for Females

	Piece	Character	Age	Playing Time
*	Agamemnon	Cassandra	20	4:15–4:45
	Iphigenia in Aulis	Iphigenia	18–20	2:00–2:15
	Antigone	Antigone	18	2:20–2:40

Monologues for Males

	The Libation Bearers	Orestes	18–20	2:20–2:40
	Hippolytus	Hippolytus	18–19	3:15–3:45
*	The Persians	Messenger	18–20	6:00–6:30

SIXTEENTH AND SEVENTEENTH CENTURIES

Monologues for Females

	Romeo and Juliet	Juliet	14	2:25–2:45
	As You Like It	Phebe	15–19	1:30–1:50
*	Life Is a Dream	Rosaura	18–21	7:00–8:00
	Le Cid	Elvire	early 20s	1:50–2:00
	The Misanthrope	Célimène	about 20	2:20–2:40

Monologues for Males

*	Life Is a Dream	Segismundo	late teens	4:15–4:45
	Henry V	King Henry	20s	3:15–3:45
*	Volpone	Volpone	early 20s	4:00–4:30
	Phaedra	Hippolytus	18–20	2:05–2:25
	Le Cid	Rodrigue	early 20s	3:20–3:50
	The Miser	Cléante	early 20s	2:15–2:35

EIGHTEENTH AND NINETEENTH CENTURIES

Monologues for Females

The Rivals	Julia	early 20s	2:00–2:20
The Contrast	Maria	18–19	1:50–2:10
The Sea Gull	Nina	18–20	1:40–1:50
The Importance of Being Earnest	Gwendolen	early 20s	1:10–1:20

Monologues for Males

Peer Gynt	Peer Gynt	about 20	2:35–2:55
* Hernani	Hernani	early 20s	4:20–4:50
Secret Service	Wilfred	16	0:50–1:10

TWENTIETH CENTURY

Monologues for Females

* Millennium	Vida Maugham	20	13:00–14:00
* Hattie B. Moore	Hattie	18	6:00–6:30
* The Misfit	Lalani	13	6:30–7:00
* Giantess	Miranda	about 20	4:30–5:00
* My Sister in This House	Lea	15	1:55–2:15
* The Monologue	Sarah	17	10:30–11:30
* Rupert's Birthday	The Woman	12–13	15:00–16:00
FOB	Grace	18–20	1:30–1:50
* American Tropical	Evelyn	18–22	5:15–5:45
* Steps	Narrator	17–18	13:00–14:00

Monologues for Males

*	Sounding Brass	Martin	19–20	7:00–7:30
*	Soldiers' Trilogy	Yonkup	17	8:40–9:10
*	The Life of the Red Hat	Patrick	18–20	10:30–11:00
	Hate Child	Charlie Bob	12	4:45–5:15
*	Delusions	John	19–20	9:00–10:00
*	The House of Blue Leaves	Ronnie	18	4:15–4:45
*	Curse of the Starving Class	Wesley	late teens	4:00–4:30
	Brontosaurus	Nephew	17–18	2:50–3:10
*	Night Walk	Carl	18–19	7:00–7:30
	Because of Romek	David	13	2:45–3:05

* Long enough to be used for some contests.

Acknowledgments

Excerpt from "Agamemnon" by Aeschylus is reprinted from THREE GREEK PLAYS, translated by Edith Hamilton, by permission of W. W. Norton & Company, Inc. Copyright 1937 by W.W. Norton & Company, Inc. renewed 1965 by Doris Fielding Reid.

Excerpt from "Iphigenia in Aulis" by Euripedes from *The Greeks: Ten Greek Plays* adapted by John Barton and Kenneth Cavander, based on original translations by Kenneth Cavander, published by Heinemann Educational Books Ltd., London, © John Barton and Kenneth Cavander, 1981.

Excerpts from "The Libation Bearers" by Aeschylus, "Hippolytus" by Euripides, and "Antigone" by Sophocles from THE COMPLETE GREEK TRAGEDIES edited by R. Lattimore and D. Grene. Copyright © 1953, University of Chicago. All rights reserved.

Excerpt from "Giantess" by Mimi Albert, published in *CrazyQuilt*, September, 1988, San Diego, and used by permission of the author.

"The Monologue" by Marla Bentz, reprinted by permission of the author.

Excerpt from "The Misfit" by Karen Carriere. First published in *CrazyQuilt*, San Diego, March 1992. Copyright © 1989 by Karen Carriere. Reprinted by permission of the author.

Excerpt from "Sounding Brass" by Marsh Cassady. Used by permission of the author.

Excerpt from "Night Walk" by Carl Catt. Used by permission of the author.

Excerpt from "Le Cid" by Corneille, as translated by Wallace Fowlie in *Classical French Drama*, published in 1962 copyright © Wallace Fowlie. Reprinted by permission of the author.

Excerpt from "The Life of the Red Hat" by Patrick Dieli. Reprinted by permission of the author.

Excerpt from "The House of Blue Leaves" by John Guare. Copyright © 1968, 1971, 1972 by St. Jude Productions, Inc. Used by permission of Viking Penguin, a division of Penguin Books USA Inc.

Excerpt from "FOB," copyright © 1979 by David Henry Hwang, from FOB AND OTHER PLAYS by David Henry Hwang. Used by permission of New American Library, a division of Penguin Books USA Inc.

"Rupert's Birthday" by Ken Jenkins is reprinted by permission of Dramatists Play Service, Inc., © Copyright 1981 by Ken Jenkins. CAUTION: The reprinting of "Rupert's Birthday" included in this volume is reprinted by permission of the owner and Dramatists Play Service, Inc. The stock and amateur performance rights in this play are controlled exclusively by Dramatists Play Service, Inc., 440 Park Avenue South, New York, NY 10016. No stock or amateur production of the play may be given without obtaining in advance, the written permission of the Dramatists Play Service, Inc., and paying the requisite fee. Inquiries concerning all other rights should be addressed to Robert A. Freedman Dramatic Agency, Inc., Suite 2310, 1501 Broadway, New York, NY 10036.

Excerpt from "My Sister in This House" by Wendy Kesselman. Copyright © 1980 by Wendy Kesselman. Reprinted by permission of the William Morris Agency, Inc. on behalf of the Author. All rights reserved. "My Sister in This House" was first produced by the Actor's Theatre of Louisville, February 1981. CAUTION: Professionals and amateurs are hereby warned that "My Sister in This House" is subject to a royalty. It is fully protected under the copyright laws of the United States of America, and of all countries covered by the International Copyright Union (including the Dominion of Canada and the rest of the British Commonwealth), and of all countries covered by the Pan-American Copyright Convention and the Universal Copyright Convention, and of all countries with which the United States has reciprocal copyright relations. All rights including professional, amateur, motion picture, recitation, lecturing, public reading, radio broadcasting, television, video or sound recording, all other forms of mechanical or electronic reproduction, such as information storage and retrieval systems and photocopying, and the rights of translation into foreign languages, are strictly prohibited. Particular emphasis is laid on the matter of readings, permission for which must be secured from the Author's agent in writing. Inquiries concerning rights should be addressed to William Morris Agency, Inc.; 1350 Avenue of the Americas; New York, NY 10019; George Lane.

Photo Credits